Into your hands

Published by The Bible Reading Fellowship
15 The Chambers, Vineyard
Abingdon OX14 3FE
United Kingdom
Tel: +44 (0)1865 319700
Email: enquiries@brf.org.uk
Website: www.brf.org.uk

ISBN 978 1 84101 587 3
First published 2008
10 9 8 7 6 5 4 3 2 1 0

Acknowledgments
Unless otherwise stated, scripture quotations are taken from The New Revised Standard Version
of the Bible, Anglicized Edition, copyright © 1989, 1995 by the Division of Christian Education
of the National Council of the Churches of Christ in the USA, and are used by permission. All
rights reserved.

Scripture quotations taken from The Revised Standard Version of the Bible, copyright © 1946,
1952, 1971 by the Division of Christian Education of the National Council of the Churches of
Christ in the United States of America, are used by permission. All rights reserved.

Scripture quotations taken from The Jerusalem Bible © 1966 by Darton, Longman & Todd Ltd
and Doubleday & Company, Inc.

Scripture quotations taken from the Holy Bible, Today's New International Version, copyright ©
2004 by International Bible Society, are used by permission of Hodder & Stoughton Publishers,
a division of Hodder Headline Ltd. All rights reserved. 'TNIV' is a registered trademark of
International Bible Society..

'The Servant King' by Graham Kendrick. Copyright ©1983 Thankyou Music. Adm. by
worshiptogether.com songs excl. UK & Europe, adm. by kingswaysongs.com tym@kingsway.
co.uk Used by permission.

'From a Distance': Words and Music by Julie Gold. Copyright © 1986, 1987 Julie Gold Music
(BMI) and Wing & Wheel Music (BMI). Julie Gold Music Administered Worldwide by Cherry
River Music Co. Wing & Wheel Music Administered Worldwide by Irving Music, Inc. Copyright
© 1986 Cherry River Music Company/Irving Music Incorporated/Wing & Wheel Music/Julie
Gold Music, USA. Rondor Music (London) Limited (50%). Used by permission of Music Sales
Limited. All rights reserved. International Copyright Secured.

Extract from Julian of Norwich, *Revelations of Divine Love*, translated into modern English by
Clifton Wolters, Penguin, 1966, used by permission of the Estate of Clifton Wolters.

Lyrics from 'Into My Arms' by Nick Cave reprinted by permission of Nick Cave and Mute Song
Limited.

Extract from *A Simple Path* by Mother Teresa, published by Rider. Reprinted by permission of
The Random House Group Ltd.

A catalogue record for this book is available from the British Library
Printed in Singapore by Craft Print International Ltd

Into your hands

Encountering the touch of God

Kevin Scully

This book is dedicated to the people and my fellow priests of the churches of St Matthew, Bethnal Green in London and St Mary, Castleton, Staten Island in New York, for whom many of these ideas and writings had their genesis.

Contents

Foreword

Christianity is a hands-on religion. While some may find themselves drawn to faith through intellectual or mystical paths, it is what happens in daily life that marks out the true believer.

We need to remember that what brings us to faith is only part of our story. What happens afterwards is how we stand out from the crowd. It has been a humbling and exciting aspect of my ministry to see so many people roll up their sleeves and get stuck into the real stuff of life around them.

Christians are involved in their daily work, in their prayerful acts of kindness and in a host of creative and social projects throughout the world. So much of what is taken for granted in some of the Western social services had their roots in Christian charity: caring for Jesus in the poor, the sick, the hungry, the thirsty and the stranger.

That is no reason for the modern believer to be complacent. There are still many challenges in our world. The God who calls us to faith also calls us to work. In small and large ways, Christians can make a difference.

In this book Kevin Scully charts a path of God's actions in the world on behalf of and through God's human creation. He takes us to the very beginning of biblical narratives to look at how the hand of God is at work in our world. He starts with an artistic image. He moves through some well- and lesser-known parts of the Bible. He also draws on a range of examples from the world of art. In all this, he suggests that what we do is tantamount to a social art.

Kevin Scully is a practical priest. I have known him since the early days of his priesthood. He has served in the inner city of London for his entire ordained ministry. In that time he has been able to produce some thoughtful books, while maintaining the practical tasks of being a Christian in the modern world.

Into Your Hands points to the way God has given us life in his created order and new life in Jesus. It also reminds us that there is a practical working out of our faith. We cannot but want to put our hands on the plough. After all, the future is in our hands as God's invited guests and friends.

John Sentamu
Archbishop of York

——— Introduction ———

The hand of God

The ceiling of the Sistine Chapel in the Vatican has one of the world's most arresting creative images. It is also perhaps one of the best-known because it dares to combine its subject with its means of execution. Creativity is used to imagine creation in the world. We start by staring up at this ceiling but end up being taken somewhere else. Michelangelo's image provides us with a fundamental link between God and humanity. The artist has portrayed the hand of God stretching out to the hand of the first human.

The image on the front cover of this book is a section of a much larger scene. The artist chose to use what many might consider an unhelpful image of an old man with a beard, more Old Father Time than the Almighty, to portray the Creator God. By looking at the hands alone, we can concentrate our thoughts on the thrust of the creation story: 'Then the Lord God formed man from the dust of the ground, and breathed into his nostrils the breath of life; and the man became a living being' (Genesis 2:7).

In the section of the picture, the finger of God is just about to touch the finger of Adam. And that touch brings no less than life into the fleshly form. That touch can be seen as the loving exchange between Creator and the created. The touch is made on the tip of a finger, the outstretched extremity of a hand.

It is no accident that the artist concentrates on the hands of both God and man. On a relatively simple level, this might be understood in the complexity of human anatomy. The hand is one of the parts of the body that distinguish *homo sapiens* from other animals. Higher primates, such as apes and chimpanzees, have the ability to grasp with both hands and feet. The structure of these parts of their anatomy is different in humans. Because of this, it can be claimed that humans are the only beings that have true hands. There are 27 bones, overlaid by a network of muscles, tendons, tissues and blood vessels all hidden from the naked eye (another complex accumulation of working cells) by skin.

It is, however, more than the intricacy of human mechanics, wonderful as they are, that is of importance. After all, the hand of God is a potentially powerful metaphor, one that can lead to sustained meditation. Of course, we do not know what God's hands would have looked like in this encounter. Many would argue that to suggest God's hands have a human form, despite God's making humans in his own image, is unhelpful. That does not mean we draw back from using the metaphor. It can be used to solemn or comic effect. The footballer Diego Maradona termed his controversial goal from a handball in the quarter-final World Cup match between England and Argentina in 1986 as 'the hand of God'. Not surprisingly, his interpretation of this event was not universally accepted.

Yet the image of the hand of God meeting humanity remains an extraordinary encounter. Michelangelo provides us with a profound theological insight in visual form. He is showing a mutuality that will become lost. The images on the chapel ceiling trace this initial reaching out from God to man to the expulsion of Adam and Eve from the garden of seeming perfection. This is a vision of what the Church calls the Fall: transgression after temptation that leads to banishment. Put simply, it is a story of creative grace being usurped. In the beginning, however, there are both a hierarchy and a potential for equality.

The hierarchy is seen in the portrayal of God, surrounded by angels in the heavenly realm, about to touch the earthbound man. It is what might be considered the distance between the eternal and the temporal. The equality is in the act of creation itself. The hand of God reaches across the chasm and gives life to humanity. In doing so, life in our hands can become Godly. This is in keeping with how the Orthodox Church seeks to explain the actions of God in Jesus: the divine became human so that humanity could become divine. It needs to be stressed that this is not based on human effort. Once again, it is the action of the Godhead that allows it.

At the point of creation there is no frustration or usurpation of that potential mutuality. That is captured in the visual wonder of the chapel, as well as in the verbal constructs of the Bible. The artist has provided a series of pictures that relate the narrative from the enlivening touch of God to a human to the expulsion from the garden of Eden.

We see what might have been—our intended destiny—when we look at the detail of Hand meeting hand. One gives to allow the other growth: the recipient reaches out to connect with the gift. Growth could find its terminus in that which led to its existence. That is the potential of creation. Much intellectual effort has been expended on trying to understand or display this potential. Yet a seemingly simple image—illusory simplicity, given the mastery of form and technique on Michelangelo's part—can encapsulate much of it.

The artist, for all the florid depiction of the creative genius of God, provides us with an image of a simple link. In this visual imagining we see established the theme that runs through so many of the early stories of the book of Genesis: God and humanity are linked. Creation is an act of consecration, never more strongly seen than in the life-giving touch of the Almighty. In this benediction we see what we are told in the first chapter of the opening book of the Bible: 'God saw everything that he had made, and indeed, it was very good' (Genesis 1:31).

This is more than some smug satisfaction on behalf of the moulder of the universe. In pronouncing it good, God has blessed the created order and thereby deemed it worthy of care. In this order we find that respect and honour are owed to creation. It may well be that, throughout Christian history, too much emphasis has been allowed to be placed on the separation between God and his creatures, captured in the doctrine of original sin, yet even that can be seen creatively. After all, we have the intellectual and imaginative gifts to deal with this and many other challenges. Such gifts can be used to good effect here. Having taken the future into their own hands, men and women lost touch with God. Much of the Bible—certainly the New Testament—concerns that separation and how it was overcome in and by Jesus.

That is a key to the Christian faith: God's hands took real human form. This is more than doctrine. For believers it is a truth captured in the link between the Creator God and Jesus, expressed in Graham Kendrick's hymn 'The Servant King':

Come see His hands
And His feet,
The scars that speak
Of sacrifice,
Hands that flung stars
Into space
To cruel nails
Surrendered.

EXTRACT TAKEN FROM 'THE SERVANT KING' BY GRAHAM KENDRICK. COPYRIGHT © 1983
THANKYOU MUSIC

It is inevitable, then, that in talking of the hand of God we will also focus on Jesus. We will consider aspects of the life of Jesus, particularly his passion and death. We will especially focus on his hands and our potential to reflect the loving responsibility of faith.

There is a good reason for this focus. The highlight of the Christian liturgical year is Holy Week. Many parts of the Church embark on a special journey of events and services that commemorate the last days of Jesus in Jerusalem. It can be a busy time for priests and people alike. So much of the faith depends on what occurs in a relatively short period. Large parts of the Gospels are given over to the passion: the betrayal, suffering and death of Jesus. Such a concentration can bring many rewards and insights.

Each of the Holy Week celebrations or services has its roots in what happened to Jesus. These events begin with the riding of the donkey into the holy city, with Jesus being greeted and applauded by people who tear palms from trees and lay down their clothes in front of the animal. The rest of the week can be given to more restrained activities. These can take many forms: special services, *agape* meals, a gathering based on the *seder* meal of the Jewish Passover, marches of witness, walking the Stations of the Cross (14 tableaux that capture the journey from Pilate's judgment to the death of Jesus on the cross and his being laid in the tomb). To that end, some of the chapters in the latter part of this book will be given over to aspects of the interplay between the hands of Jesus and his followers.

In this book the emphasis will be on the creative interchange that flows from what is a relatively small canvas, captured in one of the images of Michelangelo's expanse of ceiling: the depiction of hands. We will find connections with the Bible and with our own lives. To aid this process of making connections, there are questions and exercises that readers may want to put to themselves or discuss in a group. Each chapter concludes with a prayer.

The exchange first seen in creation is the pattern of existence: God's hand stretching out to us, and ours reaching back to God. It is the pattern of the worshipping life. Once aware of the grace of God, we seek to praise the One who blesses us in our very being. This is caught in one of the songs of Israel:

Come, bless the Lord, all you servants of the Lord,
who stand by night in the house of the Lord!
Lift up your hands to the holy place,
and bless the Lord.
May the Lord, maker of heaven and earth,
bless you from Zion. (Psalm 134)

In this we can see that all human life is touched by the hand of God. If we sense God's touch, then we can reach out towards him in meditation and prayer. It is my hope that this book will provide its readers with an opportunity to do just that, to lift hands in prayer and strive to reconnect with the outstretched, loving hand of God.

God's hands are stretched out in life and in the death of Jesus on the cross. Our hands have a faithful demand on them to respond. Sometimes that responsibility can feel overwhelming. The stretching out of hands is, in many ways, a small journey but it can point to a longer journey. Thus we will be taking a journey that repeatedly returns to the loving gesture captured in the Sistine Chapel, a gesture in which God gives life to us all.

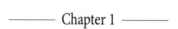

——— Chapter 1 ———

And he brought them to see what he would call them

The Bible is full of surprises but many of them can seem hidden even to regular readers. Familiarity with some parts of scripture may allow us to overlook some interesting quirks. There is one such exciting development in the second chapter of Genesis. In that version of the creation narrative, God effectively hands over the world he has made into the care of the first man. There is imaginative power in this act.

Think of a child playing with toys in a sandpit. The child's hands have moved the sand around, sculpting an environment for the toy people that are to inhabit this new world. The hands, giant-like in comparison with the tiny figures in the new landscape, place each of the figures in its allotted spot. Then the child draws back and surveys the scene. The action of withdrawal gives life to the new world. She may initiate conversations, speaking on behalf of each player in her creative drama, but she imbues each doll with a personality of its own. She is part of her own making that includes a vast distance from the mind of the creator to the action of her new world.

It is possible to discern a similar quality of play in the second creation story in Genesis. The Almighty has wrought wonders: the man has been made; the breath of life has been blown into his nostrils; a garden has been planted; knowledge of good and evil has been placed in the midst of it all; rivers flow; precious metals and jewels are embedded. Then God places man in the middle of the garden.

Then the Lord God said, 'It is not good that the man should be alone; I will make him a helper as his partner.' So out of the ground the Lord God formed every animal of the field and every bird of the air, and brought them to the man to see what he would call them; and whatever the man called each living creature, that was its name. (Genesis 2:18–19)

This is arguably the place in scripture where God hands over the created order into the stewardship of humanity. In the earlier chapter of Genesis, one that tells a different version of the creation narrative, we have been assured that God looked on all that he had made and it was very good. In the second account there is a mighty difference: God pronounces a flaw. God himself announces that there is part of his work that is not good: the created being needs a helper.

In what follows, man seeks his helpmeet. In doing so, he is given both the care and charge of all that has been made for him. God places before the man each living creature that he has formed out of ground and watches to see what the man will name them. This is a poetic variation on the charge given to the woman and man, created on the same day, destined to be equal and blessed: 'God blessed them, and God said to them, "Be fruitful and multiply, and fill the earth and subdue it; and have dominion over the fish of the sea and over the birds of the air and over every living thing that moves upon the earth"' (Genesis 1:28).

Both creation stories point to the same core message: the world has been given into the care of humanity. From this follows a host of considerations. What is the difference between dominion and domination? Does responsibility to care for other species come only because humanity is more powerful? Is it proper to prey on them, even destroy them? Is protection of the weaker beings part of the onus of dominion? What is the proper management of a world where other creatures are there expressly for the sustenance of humanity?

There are many different responses to these questions and we might not agree over our answers. Indeed, we may find ourselves arguing for seemingly irreconcilable points of view. I have witnessed such debates and it can befuddle the listener to hear the combatants appealing to the same sources, some of them biblical, to support their contradictory arguments.

The key to these complexities for believers lies in a basic premise. God has given the world into our hands. We need to try to place ourselves at some distance to comprehend the effects of our actions. We have to challenge ourselves to think outside of the world in which we live in order to understand it better. In effect, this is trying to put ourselves into an impossible viewpoint, that of God. Mystics and poets can help us here. The song 'From a distance', penned by Julie Gold but popularized by Bette Midler, provides a perspective on the earth that may not be apparent as we live and work on it. Colours, shapes, even individual and societal relationships, can be understood in a new way. The song's chorus assures us:

God is watching us, God is watching us,
God is watching us from a distance.

This sentiment can be moving when heard in its musical form but risks banality on the page. Songs make sense when they are heard.

A 14th-century mystic, Julian of Norwich, provides a useful image for us. In much the same way as we can compare the playing child to the distant God, we can look down on the world, seeing it in a hazelnut. In her *Revelations of Divine Love*, Julian wrote in perhaps her best known passage:

I saw that he is everything that we know to be good and helpful. In his love he clothes us, enfolds and embraces us; that tender love completely surrounds us, never to leave us. As I saw it he is everything that is good.

And he showed me more, a little thing, the size of a hazelnut, on the palm of my hand, round like a ball. I looked at it thoughtfully and wondered, 'What is this?' And the answer came, 'It is all that is made.' I marvelled that it continued to exist and did not suddenly disintegrate; it was so small. And again my mind supplied the answer, 'It exists, both now and forever, because God loves it.' In short, everything owes its existence to the love of God.

In this 'little thing' I saw three truths. The first is that God made it; the second is that God loves it; and the third is that God sustains it. But what he is who is in truth Maker, Keeper, and Lover I cannot tell; for until I am essentially united with him I can never have full rest or real happiness; in other words, until I am so joined to him that there is absolutely nothing between my God and me.[1]

Let us stick with the idea of the world in our hands. Of course, Julian is trying to portray an image of how God might look at his creation. It is useful that the hazelnut is pictured as being in a hand, as the hand has substantial power. The nut is removed from view by simply by making a fist around it. It can be thrown away. Or it can be brought closer to the eye of the beholder.

Julian's passage is one of reassurance and tenderness. God loves his creation and the mystic's message is that it is tenderly held in God's hand. If we think of ourselves as holding this hazelnut, being the one in authority, like the child in the sandpit mentioned earlier, we can understand the responsibility of stewardship. Having been given dominion over the earth, it is incumbent that stewardship is carried out responsibly.

Some of this responsibility lies in the nature of that over which dominion has been given. A hazelnut is fairly hardy, with an armour-like shell. Anyone who has misguidedly attempted to crack one between their teeth will know that this is not an effective method. A sturdy nutcracker or even a hammer swung on to the nutshell on a hard surface is the least force required. The kernel can be ground for culinary purposes and is used in many foods, especially sweets. It is a central ingredient of praline in some kinds of chocolate and forms the basis of the Austrian *torte*, a multi-layered cake, the ground nuts being used as an alternative to flour.

Because of its hardiness a hazelnut is a particularly apt metaphor for the world. The natural order was, for centuries, considered resilient. Humanity could make incursions into it but, if left alone, it would begin a process of recovery. Nature seemed good at renewing itself. Even major disruptions—the devastation of Flanders' fields in the First World War being one major example—could be accommodated by the earth. If left alone, it can and does begin a process of rejuvenation.

Human endeavour has imperilled that aspect of the world. The impact of human activity on the natural order is now seen as significantly and permanently damaging and this presents us with a conundrum. If creation is an ongoing matter, and many would argue that it is, then creativity has a destructive side. Each 'advance' in modern living comes at some cost.

This reflects a deep theological and natural truth. Having been given dominion over the world, humanity acts in a seemingly God-like manner: it can build up or destroy. Much of the natural order cannot compete with the effects of sustained interference. The stewardship of natural resources requires thought, effort and management. Every human action has some aftershock, even if minimal. A walk on the grass leaves imprints, a trail of minor damage. If this is random and unsustained, there is no problem. But if a route is repeatedly used, a path soon forms and the grass dies. At first this can be helpful. Those who walk in the country can discern the right of way by the path, yet it can lead to erosion, especially on popular routes. Water will channel along the path, making it deeper, and another path is made on firmer ground to one side.

The very fact of our being alive can be instructive in understanding our impact on the world. Our breath changes the make-up of the atmosphere. Too many people breathing the same air in a confined space can lead to stuffiness, a lack of oxygen and, ultimately, suffocation.

We are more familiar with considering the impact of the motor car on the environment. Land is absorbed in the building of roads. Habitats are eradicated. Species are reduced or even made extinct. The air quality in the proximity of roads degenerates. A build-up of traffic uses more fuel, thus depleting global stocks of petroleum. How many people think of this impact when they get into the car to pop down to the shops, to collect the children from school or to go to church?

Many church leaders speak of the need to care for God's creation but this does not seem to stop building schemes that require large amounts of electricity and other resources to support the latest initiative. Many new church buildings draw on fashions in other parts of the construction industry. How many church committees try to quantify the ongoing impact of a new building in terms of its electricity consumption? Is the heating of the church building efficient? Are there methods that can minimize the overall effect on natural resources?

In some congregations success is measured by the size of the car park and how quickly it fills before a service. What would happen if such churches promoted alternative transport: walking, cycling, car pooling or public transport? Are smaller, local gatherings potentially more beneficial to a greater good?

Some churches generate a new service book for every gathering. What is the cost of this in electricity? What happens to the booklets after their use? Are they thrown away or recycled? Similar questions can be asked about provision of refreshments. Are they served in reusable or in disposable cups? Has any discussion been had over where the tea or coffee comes from? Are the producers paid a fair price for their goods?

There are personal, social and political implications in the very fact of being, and the story of creation links us to them through God. People of faith need to think through these implications. They are not easy. We cannot bluff our way past them with pat answers. Dealing with them takes thought, consideration and reflection and, for people of faith, it requires prayer.

The actions of humanity lead to many consequences for the natural world. Creation has been placed into our hands. What we do with it matters.

Questions

1. What are the differences between the creation stories in the first chapters of the book of Genesis?
2. How does the second account inform our ideas on:
   ❖ our place in the world?
   ❖ our relationship with other creatures?
   ❖ differences between the sexes?
3. What are the differences between dominion and domination?
4. In what ways can we modify our lives to reflect our views on the world?
5. Who should take responsibility for the impact of lifestyles:
   ❖ in our home?
   ❖ in our workplace?
   ❖ in our church?
6. If changes could or should be made, what should take priority?

Exercises

1. Place a hazelnut or a small stone in your hand. Feel its weight. Look at it. Close your hand around it slowly and with care. Then close your hand around the nut or stone swiftly, not unduly bothering about what happens. Does the speed of these actions affect your feelings? If so, how?
2. Carry out a waste audit. See how much you throw out:
   ❖ at home.
   ❖ at work.
   ❖ from your church.
3. Read aloud the passage from Julian of Norwich in this chapter. Sit for five minutes in silence, reflecting on what she said.
4. Read the great song of creation captured in Psalm 104.

Prayer

Creator God,
you hold us and the rest of your making in your hand.
Your love for us dares to give into our hands
that which you have made.
Help us to consider the impact we have on your world.
Challenge us to look beyond our immediate needs
to see how we might fit into the web of your gift of life.
We ask this through your revealed self,
Jesus, in the sustaining life of the Spirit.
Amen

NOTES

1 Julian of Norwich, *Revelations of Divine Love*, translated into modern English by Clifton Wolters, Penguin, 1966.

⊹

——— Chapter 2 ———

Into my arms, O Lord

The story of creation tells of the defining action of God and it also reveals the nature of the Creator. God's love is such that it cannot be contained as it is poured out to make the world. This action allows the created order to respond in love to the God who lovingly made it. This can be done in many ways.

God's action is the primordial intervention. It has a peculiar power because, taken literally, God interposes into nothingness. This is captured in the first words of the Bible: 'In the beginning when God created the heavens and the earth, the earth was a formless void and darkness covered the face of the deep, while a wind from God swept over the face of the waters' (Genesis 1:1–2). His first action is active speech which has extraordinary consequences: 'Then God said, "Let there be light"; and there was light' (v. 3).

In the introduction to this book I looked at the hand of God as portrayed by Michelangelo. A traditional way of referring to God's overseeing the world and events in it is the 'hand of God': the hand of God steers his creation; events are made to happen by the hand of God; his touch is upon people.

The question as to how far God has continued or continues to intervene in the created order is a complex one. Is creation a once-only event or is it an ongoing act? Did God act and then subsequently choose certain times to intervene? Does God select moments to disrupt the established order? Other questions follow on from these ones. What powers are needed to discern God's action? What is the appropriate way of assessing such activity? Are there conditions or circumstances that somehow prioritize what God chooses to do? Who are the chosen vessels to contain such wisdom?

The questions can be reframed to use the imagery of God's hand. Has God withdrawn his hands from what he has made? Or do they still shape events? Does his finger point to certain occurrences but not to others? Does God touch someone to give them special knowledge? Does he point the way to someone by moulding what happens? Has he picked out some for special insight?

Much of the Bible is an attempt to wrestle with all or part of these questions. Such engagement is not reserved for the faithful. The seemingly most sceptical can revert to the language of faith and prayer in crises. To draw on but one of many examples, when the suicide bombers killed others with themselves in London on 7 July 2005, the words 'our thoughts and prayers go out to them' were regularly employed by politicians and other public figures, speaking of the injured and bereaved. Times of trouble galvanize the inner workings of the mind to draw on what can seem to be shrinking or limited inner resources.

On a mundane level people will ask God to intervene in their lives in what some may consider trifling matters. It may be a specific request: its concern could be material, personal or spiritual. They may pray for strength or ask something for themselves or others. It makes no difference that the matter appears of little consequence. People believe that God can be seen to influence even the most seemingly minute aspect of their lives.

Even the most avowed sceptics can find themselves appealing to the Almighty. A moving example of this is caught by Nick Cave in his song 'Into My Arms'. He has written:

I don't believe in an interventionist God
but I know, darling, that you do.
But if I did I would kneel down and ask him
not to intervene when it came to you:
not to touch a hair on your head,
to leave you as you are

and, if he felt he had to direct you,
then direct you into my arms.
Into my arms, O Lord,
into my arms.
Into my arms, O Lord,
into my arms.

Prayer can be both private and public, although some people feel less qualified than others to put their hands together in prayer. Those who exercise a prayer ministry in their church will recognize the humbling privilege of being asked to pray with or for someone. Clergy are just some of the more visible of the faithful who are regularly asked to pray for others. 'Say one for me' is a commanding request often made to priests. Sometimes the remark is said jocularly but it almost always stems from a serious intent. People believe that God is concerned for them and that, in some way, God listens to the 'experts'. Those who field the request usually have a less elevated view of their own faculties. The most devoted pray-er will probably claim no more than amateur status.

The term 'answer to prayer' is not the most helpful. When people say that their prayers have been answered, they often mean that they got what they desired. That may not be the best test of prayer. Openness to God's will must allow for the possibility that we do not always get what we consider the best for ourselves or others.

One of the most startling examples of spiritual insight I encountered came from a woman telling a group of fellow Christians about the time when her husband suffered a fatal heart attack in front of her. He dropped dead in their home. She prayed fearfully and urgently that this man, the father of their teenage son, would come back to life. Despite the arrival of the ambulance crew and their emergency procedures his heart did not resume its beat. 'I was angry. I was distraught. I wanted him to live. But it was not to be. And I had prayed. It was hard. It took a long time for me to understand that "no" was also an answer to prayer.'

One attitude to prayer which is heard from time to time amounts to an attack on a person's faith. This is the view that if we do not get what we have asked for, we lack appropriate faith. Such an attitude can cause great damage. It corrupts the advice of Jesus who, while saying we should ask to receive, painted a broader picture of demand and receipt in the Lord's Prayer. An instructive model of prayer can be seen in the petition of Solomon, when he asks that what is bestowed on him would be to the benefit of others.

God answered Solomon, 'Because this was in your heart, and you have not asked for possessions, wealth, honour, or the life of those who hate you, and have not even asked for long life, but have asked for wisdom and knowledge for yourself that you may rule my people over whom I have made you king, wisdom and knowledge are granted to you.' (2 Chronicles 1:11–12)

It is only after this that Solomon learns that he may also benefit materially. Solomon's request is the equivalent of opening his hands to God and God chooses to fill them to overflowing.

Prayer is perhaps best seen as an inclination of the heart. We open ourselves to God to allow God to move us. We effectively meet God with empty hands so that he can do with them what he wills. This can be done if we follow the suggestion of Jesus: 'Go into your room and shut the door and pray to your Father who is in secret; and your Father who sees in secret will reward you' (Matthew 6:6).

Prayer also has a community focus. There has been a marked recovery in communal prayer in some churches in recent years. Many have learned of the benefits to be gained in prayers that have their basis in monastic offices. The offices are mainly set prayers, usually drawn heavily from the Psalms, that are offered when monks and nuns stop work at various points of the day and night to pray. People beyond the cloister may come together on weekdays in many churches for morning or evening prayer. This can include recitation of Psalms, readings from the Old and New Testaments and set prayers. It also allows for a quiet time of collective contemplation.

Public prayer can take many forms. Perhaps the most familiar one is a designated time of prayer or intercession during a church service. Those who lead this time fulfil an important and responsible ministry within their worshipping community. One London church, in its preparation for those who lead the prayers of the people at its Sunday service, advises that the best preparation for prayer is prayer itself. The guidelines from St Matthew's, Bethnal Green, offer the following tips:

- Don't tell God what to think or do—it is better to hold people and issues before God—it is usually better to pray *for* rather than *that…*
- Don't be too particular in directing God's attention to things— 'Lord, as you will have seen on page three of the paper', 'Paradoxical as it may seem to you, Lord…'
- Allow space, time and silence. People need time to connect with where you are leading them. They also have their own concerns, worries, intentions. It is best to acknowledge that.

Prayer is a sign of faith. Simply, it is a way of putting our life and concerns into the hands of God. It may not be a consistent practice in some people's lives but the fact that they resort to it in a crisis should not be dismissed or belittled, but rather welcomed, by people of faith. Part of the pilgrimage of faith is realizing that there is not one template for all people in coming to see the relationship between the creative, loving God who reaches out to them and their own circumstances.

Prayer can involve hands. Gesture can enhance it. The hands can be raised into the air or pressed hard into each other. Fingers tell the beads of rosaries or count off the notches of a prayer rope. Foreheads can be contained in cupped hands. The hands can be open as a flower or formally held in the pose of the ubiquitous praying hands seen in the drawing by Albrecht Dürer. Many who exercise a prayer ministry will lay their hands on those for whom they pray, symbolizing the link between God and his creation. This has particular resonance when the prayer is offered for healing. Paul has advice for members of the early Church: 'I desire, then, that in every place the men should pray, lifting up holy hands without anger or argument' (1 Timothy 2:8).

On a profound level a Christian has no option but to declare that God does interact with his creation, because the Gospels provide various accounts of the most radical intervention by God in the miracles of Jesus. This is reflected in Christian doctrine and worship, above all in the incarnation of God taking human form. 'And the Word became flesh and lived among us, and we have seen his glory, the glory as of a father's only son, full of grace and truth' (John 1:14). The Almighty comes to be seen in the form of a human baby. The omnipotent creator of the world chooses to become a helpless infant as Jesus, the child of Mary.

People often comment on the marvel of a newborn child's hands. All that is required is there in miniature. They simply lack the coordination to do anything of practical use. Jesus shared that quality with all babies. At birth he could not feed himself, keep himself warm or even clean himself. A baby is literally placed into the hands of another, usually the mother. Mary and Joseph were charged with a supernatural task when the baby Jesus was placed into their hands for human nurture. A great deal is to be drawn from this conundrum of the all-powerful in a state of voluntary powerlessness. We can then ponder on Jesus coming to learn of the dexterity and restriction of human movement, while later using his hands to heal and cast out demons. These are the same hands that offer healing to the world by being nailed to the cross.

It is this link between the Godly and the human, when God's hands took the form of a human's, that can encourage us to place our concerns into the hands of God. It is also appropriate that when Christians pray they make their prayer through Jesus.

God chose what is low and despised in the world, things that are not, to reduce to nothing things that are, so that no one might boast in the presence of God. He is the source of your life in Christ Jesus, who became for us wisdom from God, and righteousness and sanctification and redemption, in order that, as it is written, 'Let the one who boasts, boast in the Lord.' (1 Corinthians 1:28–31)

While the faithful acknowledge, as it says in the Athanasian Creed, that 'none is afore or after' in the Trinity—there being one eternal, one Almighty, one God and one Lord—we connect to the hand of God that reached out in human form in the person of Jesus.

Prayer is often the best way to prepare for reading the Bible. It centres our minds and can incline our hearts to God's heart. It is a way not so much of grabbing what we can as allowing our hearts and minds to be placed into God's open hands.

Questions

1. At what times in your life have you felt close to God?
2. What circumstances have ever led you to think God might be directing your actions?
3. What have been the times in your life when God felt far away from you?
4. How has your experience of prayer been changed or affected by the changes or events in your life?
5. Do you have a preferred way of praying? What is it? Why?

Exercises

1. How do you hold your hands when you pray? Let your hands assume their normal shape. Look at them. If you are in a group, show one another. Do you do this because someone showed you? Who was it? When did you adopt what you were shown?
2. Try placing your hands in one of the following prayer poses:
   - ❖ Raise your hands in the air.
   - ❖ Cup your forehead in your hands.
   - ❖ Place the back of your hands on your thighs, palms turned upwards.
   - ❖ Hold them in Albert Dürer's classic *Praying Hands* position.
   Discuss anything you noticed from doing this.

3. Assume a hand position for prayer that is not your normal one. Make sure it is one that you can hold for some time. Sit in silence for five minutes.
4. If you are members of a group, lay hands on each other. (It may be best to split into units of no more than five people or pairs if yours is a large group.) You can ask if there is a specific request or concern, then simply offer that request to God on behalf of the other person.

Prayer

O Creator God,
whose hands have formed us from eternity:
we place into your hands
our thoughts, our beings and our actions
so that we can be shaped by your will
into the form of eternity.
We ask this in the power of the Holy Spirit,
through Jesus Christ,
one Lord, one God,
now and forever.
Amen

✤

——— Chapter 3 ———

Behold the handmaid of the Lord

As we have already seen, the Christian faith is based on the most extraordinary event: the divine took a human form. The hand of God moved from the metaphorical to the literal, meaning that God had real hands.

It also means that people saw God. This turns on its head what God told Moses when he said, 'You cannot see my face; for no one shall see me and live' (Exodus 33:20). Some people did see God, albeit in human form, in the person of Jesus. He was a real man in a real place in a real time. It is the same John, if we assume the author of the epistles to be the Gospel writer, who claims to have been a primary witness to the life, death and resurrection of Jesus (John 21:24). He seemingly contradicts himself to make this point: 'No one has ever seen God; if we love one another, God lives in us, and his love is perfected in us' (1 John 4:12).

The claim that people did see God and live is contained in much of the Church's teaching and ceremonies. As it says in one of the current series of eucharistic prayers of the Church of England, Jesus 'lived on earth and went about among us' (Prayer B). For some that is too much to contemplate. It is no real surprise, then, that Jesus should be considered both the cornerstone of the faith and a stumbling block.

A later chapter of this book will be devoted to how the hands of Jesus, and the amazing events that flowed from them, caused a revolution in his own historical time and thereafter. His touch could change lives. It could heal. It could also outrage. This chapter will concentrate on the build-up to those events. It will look at how his hands came into being in the person of another human, his mother Mary.

The hand of God was upon Mary as soon as she saw his messenger. The angel Gabriel is often portrayed in paintings of the scene as a winged courier. This may be argued as the zenith or the nadir of imagination. Angels are messengers from God so they might not look like anything we recognize. Over the years, however, a form emerged to stand for such emissaries. The fresh-faced, usually white-clad, winged and sometimes flying humanoid became the image to alert the viewer that the being was not really mortal. Whatever the angel's form, the words 'Greetings, favoured one! The Lord is with you' (Luke 1:28) were enough to frighten the young woman in Nazareth named Mary. 'But she was much perplexed by his words and pondered what sort of greeting this might be' (v. 29).

The angel is often portrayed with one hand pointing towards heaven, his fingers akin to the shape of a priestly blessing. The other hand, in a combination of election and seeming threat, points at the young woman. Mary is often slightly recoiling, her hands folded over her breast, as if to protect herself from the enormity of both the blessing and the task she has been given. When she accepts the task with the words, 'Behold, I am the handmaid of the Lord; let it be to me according to your word' (Luke 1:38, RSV), it is not without risk to herself. Mary herself questions the angel as to how his prediction may be fulfilled, as she has had no sexual experience.

Mary's actions set her on a path of great potential danger. A betrothed young woman, pregnant before her marriage, was one to whom hands would be raised. Fingers would be pointed in accusation. Indeed, under the law, hands could legitimately hurl stones at her as an adulterer. The law gave the community the power to stone her to death.

It is intriguing, then, that there is no mention of her betrothed, Joseph, and his possible reaction to this event in the Gospel of Luke. Joseph is first mentioned in relationship to Mary before the episode involving the angelic visitor. His name does not crop up again until Luke relates the happenings in Bethlehem, where Joseph had taken Mary as part of the census ordered by Caesar Augustus.

The only biblical thread to look at the plight of Joseph on hearing the news is in the Gospel of Matthew. Mary 'was found to be pregnant' (Matthew 1:18, TNIV). Joseph is variously described as just, righteous or as a man of principle. It is significant that the Gospel mentions little of how he felt about his own reputation. What it does note is that he chooses not to bring dishonour on Mary. It is only after he has made that compassionate decision that he is visited by the angel in a dream. The care of Mary and her son is placed into his hands (vv. 20–25).

There is another significant event that stems from Joseph's compassionate actions. His betrothed removes herself from the scrutiny of those among whom she lives and journeys to visit her cousin Elizabeth, who has also found herself pregnant against her own and others' expectations.

This encounter is known in the Church as the Visitation. Along with the words of the angel Gabriel at the Annunciation, Elizabeth's greeting is remembered in the first section of the prayer known as the Hail Mary. The incident is also enshrined in a place of pilgrimage. At the Church of the Visitation in Ein Karem, near Jerusalem, is a statue of unusual power. It depicts the arrival of the Virgin Mary at the home of Elizabeth. The statue is composed of the two women, each of them clearly pregnant, reaching out to place a hand on the other's enlarged belly. In the biblical account it is the child in Elizabeth's womb who alerts her to the significance of Mary's presence.

In those days Mary set out and went with haste to a Judean town in the hill country, where she entered the house of Zechariah and greeted Elizabeth. When Elizabeth heard Mary's greeting, the child leapt in her womb. And Elizabeth was filled with the Holy Spirit and exclaimed with a loud cry, 'Blessed are you among women, and blessed is the fruit of your womb. And why has this happened to me, that the mother of my Lord comes to me? For as soon as I heard the sound of your greeting,

the child in my womb leapt for joy. And blessed is she who has believed
that there would be a fulfilment of what was spoken to her by the Lord.'
(Luke 1:39–45)

The child, who cannot speak as he is still in the amniotic sac in
his mother's womb, does communicate. He joins with Elizabeth to
acclaim the arrival of Jesus in their midst. The statue at Ein Karem
has four invisible hands—those of the children—in addition to the
hands of the women that reach to each other in a compassionate
greeting.

The significance of the women and their hands continues well
after this encounter. The Gospel of Luke is the only one that contains
what is known as the birth narrative. It is the only mention in the
New Testament of the census ordered by Augustus Caesar under the
stewardship of Quirinius. Mary finds herself in less than commodious
accommodation—there was no room for them at the inn—and gives
birth to her first child.

In many pictures—illuminated manuscripts, paintings, perhaps
most famously in a Giotto fresco in the Scrovegni chapel in Padua—
there is another woman at the scene. Sometimes there are two of
them. These are the midwives who assisted Mary in the delivery of
her son. There is no biblical source for this, though they do figure
in non-canonical writings. It is helpful to realize that Mary would
almost certainly have had the support and care of other women in
her labour, in strong contrast with medieval teaching that Jesus was
born without labour pains. Such a claim has a distancing effect in that
it elevates Mary beyond all trace of common humanity. By placing
other women at the scene, the story of the incarnation becomes both
communal and tactile.

Over time one of these women even came to acquire a name.
She is called Salome and conjecture has it that the midwife who
was present at the birth of Jesus was also a witness to his death and
resurrection (Mark 15:40; 16:1). As one of the women who went to
the tomb to anoint Jesus, she acquires sainthood within some parts
of the Church.

Let our focus return to the beginning of the life of Jesus. Let us also suppose that the apocryphal story of Joseph running to enlist the assistance of a midwife for Mary in Bethlehem is true. The newborn Jesus was received into the hands of a woman. This continues the important link between God and humanity through the agency of women. The midwives would have attended to the afterbirth, the cutting of the umbilical cord, the initial washing of the baby.

The Bible tells us that Mary wrapped her baby in swaddling clothes. If we presume that Mary was alone, her own hands would have caught the child as he emerged into the world and the tasks that I have ascribed to the midwives would have been carried out by her.

In whatever account we choose, we have the strength of the incarnation becoming real. God, having taken human form, is born into the world and is literally taken into the hands of a woman. These hands take the helpless almighty one, wash him, rock him to sleep, hold him and keep him safe. His mother's hands also place him at her breast to be fed. Metaphor becomes the doctrinal reality: 'And the Word became flesh and lived among us' (John 1:14).

This has consequences, bringing a responsibility to bear on all those who are born. It is enshrined in the fifth of the Ten Commandments or captured more prosaically in the book of Ecclesiasticus in the Apocrypha:

With all your heart honour your father,
never forget the birthpangs of your mother.
Remember that you owe your birth to them;
how can you repay them for what they have done for you?
(Ecclesiasticus 7:27–28, JB)

The nativity of Jesus is often at risk of being sanitized beyond belief. We are distracted by an amalgam of angels, shepherds, wise men and farmyard onlookers from the bloody glory of childbirth. The Psalms often refer to the pains of childbirth, which was a more public event in New Testament times than for those who live in developed nations today. Birth, however, remains a hands-on affair. The power of the incarnation, of God taking the human form, is that he is received into the hands of humanity.

It seems almost comical to state that Jesus is the cornerstone of the Christian faith: that should go without saying. But then the cornerstone is also the stumbling block. If Christians dared not to sentimentalize the events of the pregnancy of Mary and the birth of her son, as in the perennial pre-Christmas infant school nativity play, many would be able to see the reality of God crossing what they consider an impassable border.

For all that, the stumbling block is actually a person. The person of Jesus is important because it was God who put himself into the hands of humanity. He made us and then gave himself to us. The intellectual puzzle of the Almighty becoming helpless is extended to and complicated by the end of the life of Jesus. Not only did God become human but he died.

For since, in the wisdom of God, the world did not know God through wisdom, God decided, through the foolishness of our proclamation, to save those who believe. For Jews demand signs and Greeks desire wisdom, but we proclaim Christ crucified, a stumbling-block to Jews and foolishness to Gentiles, but to those who are the called, both Jews and Greeks, Christ the power of God. (1 Corinthians 1:21–24)

The wonder of this gift of God in human form is perhaps best illustrated by the incident when the child is placed in the hands of an old man in the temple, when Joseph and Mary take Jesus there to offer 'a sacrifice according to what is stated in the law of the Lord, "a pair of turtle-doves or two young pigeons"' (Luke 2:24).

Simeon was guided by the Spirit to come into the temple at that time and, when he sees the baby Jesus, he takes the child from the parents and pronounces the prayer known as the Nunc Dimittis (Latin for the opening words of the prayer 'Now dismiss…'), which is used at the last prayer service of the day in many churches and religious houses. In the prayer Simeon praises God for showing to him the Saviour of the nations, a light to the people of Israel and the rest of the world. In a simple reduction of his elevated praise, he might be saying, 'I am so happy, I could die.'

Certainly his view on the special nature of the baby is confirmed by a woman. The aged prophet Anna also begins to praise God and tell everyone that the redemption of Israel is to be found in this child. Their future has been placed into their hands.

Questions

1. How do we recognize the message of God today:
   - ❖ in the world?
   - ❖ in our community?
   - ❖ in the Church?
   - ❖ in our lives?
2. Can you think of a place in the Bible where it tells of someone encountering God? What do we understand when it describes someone as 'seeing' God?
3. What can we learn from the reaction of Mary to the message of the angel:
   - ❖ in our lives?
   - ❖ in the Church?
   - ❖ in our community?
   - ❖ in the world?
4. What is your favourite part of the biblical accounts of the birth of Jesus? Why?

Exercises

Find one image each of the Annunciation and the Visitation. You may want to download and print them from a website. Pass each picture round and consider the following questions.

1. Who is the central player in the scene?
2. What might be understood from the hands:
   - ❖ of the central player?
   - ❖ of any others?
3. What can be read from the body language of:
   - ❖ the central player?
   - ❖ any others?
4. Where is the focus of attention in the picture?
5. Try to imagine yourself in the picture. What do you see yourself doing?

Prayer

God, who was content to deliver yourself
into the hands of caring women;
put into our hands and hearts
a sense of your vulnerable majesty
revealed in the shape of a baby,
even Jesus Christ our Lord.
Amen

❖

——— Chapter 4 ———

He touched her and the fever left her

The hands are the most adaptable part of the body. They can grasp and hold objects in their grip. They can twist, hold on to something and let it go. Hands can be used to do all sorts of things: play music, manipulate tools, type, use a mobile phone, pull the trigger on a gun. They can also be used to great effect. They can be used to heal.

It is a human wonder that healing hands often use very little pressure. Nor do they always require great skill or training. Think of the gentle touch of a mother on the fevered brow of her child, or of one person holding the hand of another in a simple act of sympathy. A person in emotional distress can receive great comfort from a light touch on the back, shoulder or knee from a close friend. It conveys more than words could capture.

There is also the wonderful power of trained hands: the reassuring hands of a doctor examining a nervous patient; the adjusting movements of a physiotherapist, chiropractor or osteopath; the skilled use of the hands by a dentist or surgeon; the intense actions of the hands of a masseur. Pressure, sustained effort and release can be used to relieve all sorts of ailments. In all these diverse areas the hands and fingers are the tangible extension of education, training and experience.

The New Testament is full of stories of the most powerful hands, for a believer. Jesus turned his hands to the service of others and the results were truly miraculous. The Gospels contain many incidents when Jesus simply extends his hands in a light touch to effect a cure that stuns both the person who has come to him and those who witness the healing. A number of times his touch brings even brings somebody back from the dead. Little wonder that people wanted to see him.

The best way to learn of the wonder of the healing hands of Jesus is to read the Gospel writers' accounts of them. This chapter will look at a few incidents recorded in the Gospels, a limited selection from a far larger number of healing incidents.

Let us start with the most amazing of all: the touch of Jesus that literally restores life to the dead. There are three occasions where this miracle is recorded in the Gospels: the raising of the daughter of Jairus in Matthew, Mark and Luke; the widow's son at Nain told in the Gospel of Luke; and the raising of Lazarus in the Gospel of John. The latter story, wonderful as it is, will not be part of our reflections here because the incident precludes Jesus' touching anyone or anything as he draws his friend back to life. Rather, he calls out to Lazarus from outside the tomb and then he instructs others to unbind him and let him go (John 11:1–44).

The story of the widow's son at Nain appears in Luke 7:11–17, a section that contains a number of incidents in which Jesus associates with those whom many would consider beyond the pale for social or religious reasons: a Roman centurion, a dead person and a sinful woman. It is the second event that concerns us.

The death of the woman's husband and son leaves her abandoned and possibly destitute. Unless her husband had provided for her, she would be at risk of having to rely on the charity of others. As the dead body of the young man is being carried out of the city gate to burial, Jesus surveys the scene. 'When the Lord saw her, he had compassion for her and said to her, "Do not weep." Then he came forward and touched the bier, and the bearers stood still' (Luke 7:13–14a).

It is only after his touch has brought the procession to a halt that Jesus speaks. 'And he said, "Young man, I say to you, rise!" The dead man sat up and began to speak, and Jesus gave him to his mother' (v. 15).

Those who witness this are rightly amazed. The consequence is that they begin to praise God. How would people respond to such an event today? I suspect there would be a sense of healthy cynicism, a wondering about what kind of trick might be involved. No such doubts are recorded in the Gospel account. People see a light touch on the bier bringing a man back to life. They realize that power does not necessarily coexist with huge effort.

The other restoration of life, to the daughter of Jairus, also follows the actions of the hands of Jesus. The longest account of this event is also recorded in Luke's Gospel. In this version Jairus, a leader of the synagogue, falls at the feet of Jesus as he is making his way home from the strange events in the country of the Gerasenes (8:26–39). A crazed man has been restored to his right mind, and spirits that tormented him have entered some pigs, which have run down a bank and drowned themselves in the lake.

Jairus begs Jesus to come to the house where his daughter—again, an only child—is dying. On the way another extraordinary event, to which we will return shortly, occurs. For the moment let us stick with the narrative of the young girl, which Luke chooses to interrupt.

Someone from the house of Jairus arrives and breaks the news that the girl, of about twelve years in age, has died. The writer of Luke tells us that three disciples, Peter, John and James, were the witnesses of what happened when Jesus got to the house. He told the grieving family and friends to stop crying, '"... for she is not dead but sleeping." And they laughed at him, knowing that she was dead. But he took her by the hand and called out, "Child, get up!" Her spirit returned, and she got up at once' (8:52–55).

Another story of healing, though not one of resurrection, has particular power because of the theme of this book. In this encounter, the hand of Jesus stretches out to restore wholeness to the hand of another. It is not the healing in itself that attracts the attention of the author of Luke's Gospel. It is the fact that the healing occurs on a certain day of the week and is part of a train of events that leads to Jesus being condemned by the religious leaders of the day. He was condemned because he seemed to ignore the rules of the faith by curing people's illnesses on the sabbath.

The writer of Luke has just told how the followers of Jesus plucked heads of grain and rubbed them in their hands as they walked through a field on the sabbath. Luke goes on to say that Jesus went into a synagogue and started teaching. Among the people was a man whose right hand was withered. The scribes and Pharisees, keen to find something over which to accuse Jesus, watched to see if he would cure on the sabbath (6:6–8). Jesus called the man forward and, as the man stood in front of him, he asked his would-be accusers if it was lawful to cure people on the sabbath. 'After looking around at all of them, he said to him, "Stretch out your hand." He did so, and his hand was restored. But they were filled with fury and discussed with one another what they might do to Jesus' (vv. 10–11).

There are many other examples of Jesus touching people and curing them: he touches the tongue and places his fingers in the ears of a man who cannot hear or speak (Mark 7:33); he mixes a paste from dirt to restore another man's sight (John 9:6); he extends his hand to the boy who suffers from what many believe was epilepsy (Mark 9:27). Jesus also visits the mother-in-law of Peter when she lies ill in bed. 'He touched her hand, and the fever left her, and she got up and began to serve him' (Matthew 8:15).

All these incidents—and many others—involve Jesus touching others and they recover. The Gospels repeatedly record that there was power in the hands of Jesus.

Mention has been made of another incident that interrupts the narrative of the miracle of bringing Jairus' daughter back from the dead. It involves a woman who reaches out to Jesus and touches his cloak. She was suffering from a long-term issue of blood, a gynaecological condition that would have made her a social and religious pariah, preventing physical contact with others. 'Now there was a woman who had been suffering from haemorrhages for twelve years; and though she had spent all she had on physicians, no one could cure her' (Luke 8:43).

The woman has used the cover of a large crowd to press in on Jesus and, hoping that he will not notice, she reaches out and touches him. The effect is immediate and startling. By merely brushing the fringe of his clothes with her fingers, she is healed. The bleeding stops. 'Then Jesus asked, "Who touched me?" When all denied it, Peter said, "Master, the crowds surround you and press in on you." But Jesus said, "Someone touched me; for I noticed that power had gone out from me"' (vv. 45–46).

The now healed woman was hoping to keep her cure a secret but Jesus does not let the matter drop. In the end, the woman steps forward.

When the woman saw that she could not remain hidden, she came trembling; and falling down before him, she declared in the presence of all the people why she had touched him, and how she had been immediately healed. He said to her, 'Daughter, your faith has made you well; go in peace.' (vv. 47–48)

There can be no doubt of the power that flows from the hands of Jesus. There is gentleness and healing but there is also a power to rebuke and challenge. Two incidents of a very different nature should suffice to undergird this point. When the woman caught in adultery is brought to him, Jesus hesitates before saying anything. He bends down and draws in the dirt. There have been several speculations about this: he was doodling while thinking of what he was to say; he was pretending to ignore the crowd of men who had come to accuse and perhaps stone to death the woman; he was writing out the sins of those who made up the posse.

All this was a prelude to words of challenge and comfort: 'Let anyone among you who is without sin be the first to throw a stone at her' (John 8:7). Jesus then bends down to write in the dirt again. While he is doing this, the woman's accusers leave one by one. Eventually she is left alone with Jesus. 'Jesus straightened up and said to her, "Woman, where are they? Has no one condemned you?" She said, "No one, sir." And Jesus said, "Neither do I condemn you. Go your way, and from now on do not sin again"' (vv. 10–11).

The second incident is dramatic. Arriving at the temple, the holiest site for the Jewish people, Jesus becomes enraged. He rebukes those who have established a trade in the necessities of worship, the supply of sacrificial animals. He also turns on those who trade in cash. The hands of Jesus are turned to stormy action. 'Making a whip of cords, he drove all of them out of the temple, both the sheep and the cattle. He also poured out the coins of the money-changers and overturned their tables' (John 2:15).

We can dare to see the whole character of Jesus through his hands. The seemingly contradictory elements of gentleness and rebuke, healing and challenge, combine in one encounter. As in the stories of the birth of Jesus, we should exercise caution in case we end up with an image that does not contain the breadth of human experience and emotions.

The action of healing also involves one of intent. People travelled to see Jesus. They reached out to him in the hope or belief that he could make them well again. There is both activity and reception involved. In many ways, that is what we do when we pray ourselves or when we seek the healing power of Christ through the ministry of the Church. Many churches provide special services of prayer, meditation and healing as part of their ministry and this can involve the laying of hands or anointing.

Those who came to Jesus reached out to him and he reached out to them. These complementary actions are worth keeping in mind. Part of the walk of faith is being prepared to admit our need for help. By asking and receiving we ensure that a blessed reciprocity continues. In this way the grace of God cannot be contained or dammed but overflows to those who need it.

This also presents a challenge. Jesus tells his followers that they must be prepared to give when they are asked for assistance. In this way they become agents of God's work, charged with carrying on his healing work. It is an awesome responsibility.

'God has no hands but our hands,' Teresa of Avila is quoted as saying. Do we dare to allow ourselves to consider our hands as God's hands? Is it possible that the hands that offer us comfort or rebuke are being used by God? Or do we limit such activity to a holy huddle in church (important though that can be)?

Jesus made the point that healing can come from surprising

quarters. The parable of the good Samaritan (Luke 10:30–35) shows someone reaching over societal boundaries to offer care to someone in genuine need. Indeed, Jesus asks the lawyer whose question led to the parable to identify who was the neighbour to the injured man. The answer was, of course, the Samaritan, not the priest or Levite as might have been expected. Furthermore, Jesus says, 'Go and do likewise' (v. 37).

Questions

1. What is your favourite account of the healing ministry of Jesus? Why?
2. Which stories of the healing miracles of Jesus have puzzled you? Why?
3. Have there been times in your life when you feel God has blessed you with his healing power? How did this happen? Were other people involved?
4. Tell each other any instances when you have felt close to God:
   - ❖ through the ministry of the Church.
   - ❖ through the work of a doctor, or practitioner in complementary or alternative health services.

Exercises

1. Members of the group can lay hands on each other. This can be done in turn, or in a number of small groups, or simply by holding hands in a circle. It is worth keeping silent for at least three minutes. If members of the group are unfamiliar with such activity, it may be best to stop there and discuss how it felt.
2. If members agree to it, people can ask for a special prayer—for themselves or others—to be offered during the time of silence. The exercise can end with the following prayer.

Prayer

In the name of the healing God,
present in the hands of our Lord Jesus Christ,
and by his grace among us now,
receive his comfort and care
so that you may be made whole
in body, mind and spirit.
Amen

⁘

─────── Chapter 5 ───────

God has no hands but our hands

'God has no hands but our hands.' In this chapter I want to reflect on this saying, attributed to St Teresa of Avila, a 16th-century Spanish mystic, which I mentioned towards the end of the previous chapter. Teresa was also the founder of a number of relatively strict convents of contemplative nuns. A version of the saying has also been attributed to another woman who lived some five centuries after the Spanish Carmelite. She was also a nun—Mother Teresa of Calcutta. This Albanian-born sister was famous for her devoted and prayerful action in bringing God's love to the forgotten poor.

The saying 'God has no hands but our hands' captures a profound essence of Christian living. Faith is a response to God's love: the knowledge that God loves us changes us. Having become aware of the change, action follows. This is how God's hands continue to work in the world through our hands. It has its extension in those bracing words from the letter of James where he urges the followers of Jesus to act on their faith.

But be doers of the word, and not merely hearers who deceive themselves. For if any are hearers of the word and not doers, they are like those who look at themselves in a mirror; for they look at themselves and, on going away, immediately forget what they were like. But those who look into the perfect law, the law of liberty, and persevere, being not hearers who forget but doers who act—they will be blessed in their doing. (James 1:22–25)

Holy Week is the time above all others in the Church's year when we see this love acted out through the hands of Jesus. On Palm Sunday

Christians set out on the prayerful handiwork that is Holy Week.

Indeed, the celebrations on Palm Sunday are just the first of a number of set pieces:

- Maundy Thursday, with its re-enactment of the washing of the disciples' feet by Jesus, the meal in which Jesus ordered his followers to remember him in the breaking of the bread, the stripping of the altars and the meditative watch recalling the agonizing hours in the garden of Gethsemane.
- Good Friday, with the bare church, the veneration of the cross, and a simple Communion service in pared-down ritual.
- The Easter Vigil, in which the scriptures of anticipation are read by candlelight in darkened churches before an explosion of light to celebrate the light of Christ triumphing over the darkness of the world. This follows on to a renewal of baptismal promises to follow Jesus.
- The beginning of the ongoing festival that is Easter.

In many churches parts of palm trees are distributed, blessed and carried in a march of witness around the local area. When that happens our hands become instruments of action. We take hold of our palm crosses, clutching them in the palms of our own hands, grasping the symbol of our salvation.

In sign language, the sign for 'tree' is the same on both sides of the Atlantic—in BSL, the sign language used in Britain, and ASL, American Sign Language. The length of the arm from the elbow to the wrist signifies the trunk. In the hand we see the boughs and the leaves. Sign language dictionaries tell us that the fingers can wiggle to indicate a leaf moving in the wind. Sign language is an iconic language: that is, it sometimes mirrors the shape of an object to express it. Clearly, in this sign, the hands take the form of the word.

It is worth spending some time with the word 'palm'. *The Concise Oxford Dictionary of English Etymology*, which looks at the origins of over 17,000 words, tells us that the English word comes from *palma* in Latin. The definition establishes a link between the word we use for the palm of the hand and a tree. It says this: 'part of the trunk of a tree from which the branches spring'.[1] As such, it designates 'palms' as the limbs of trees in general, as well as the specific genus of the palm tree.

Where might this information of word and sign take us? In worship we hope that we are building some sort of holy community. It is an activity through which many seek to join together to express a realization of God's love. In doing this, the people of the church place their lives before God while offering thanks and praise for what God has done for the world in the person of Jesus. For a believer this activity is also personal. What is being said collectively is true for the individual: I celebrate what God has done for me in the person of Jesus. That is what the story of Holy Week is about. The carrying of a palm in our hands is both a personal and corporate act: in the same way that individual palms come from one tree, we are individual members of the Church.

Paul, in the first letter to Timothy (1:4), gives advice to the people about how the church should worship God. He has been telling them that their faith should affect the way they live in the real world. It should not be all about ideas and high falutin' thinking. This kind of advice then becomes concrete in his views on how people (at least, the men) should worship, as he says, 'I desire, then, that in every place the men should pray, lifting up holy hands without anger or argument' (2:8).

We can take this advice too far because Paul then goes on to say a lot of things that many believers might not agree with, or may question how to understand (to mention but one—how women should dress and conduct themselves, especially in relation to authority in the church). This is both a historical and a contemporary issue that gives rise to friction among people in the Church.

But let us return to the hands. The author of the letter says that they are to be lifted, without rancour or dissension, in praise to God. That is one way of looking at the events of Palm Sunday. For one part of that special week of Christian worship and commemoration, the faithful unite in their journey along with Jesus. They act as one. Their hands become at one with branches of trees, waved aloft in worship to accompany the triumphal entrance of Jesus into Jerusalem.

Many churches have a special procession as a march of witness on Palm Sunday. That procession is usually preceded by a reading from one of the Gospels, relating how branches were torn from trees and placed, along with people's cloaks, in front of a colt on which Jesus rode into the holy city. That procession was seen as a fulfilment of a prophecy that the Messiah, drawn from the line of David, would enter Jerusalem riding on a young donkey.

Rejoice greatly, O daughter Zion!
Shout aloud, O daughter Jerusalem!
Lo, your king comes to you;
triumphant and victorious is he,
humble and riding on a donkey,
on a colt, the foal of a donkey. (Zechariah 9:9)

Those who take part in such processions become actors in a kind of memorial pageant through the streets of their community. They often capture a sense of excitement that regular church services lack. Some even employ the services of a real donkey. Gathering in a place other than the church gives a relaxed, festive air to the proceedings. Palms range from branches of trees to small pieces of palms folded into the shape of a cross.

Those who march around their local areas, or from church to church, hold these large and miniature arboreal palms in the palms of their hands, using them to remember the palms taken from the trees of Jerusalem and placed in front of Jesus. We can also envisage a symbolic transfer being enacted. Their hands are full, if only for a moment, to show that God has come to earth. They enact this by taking the branches from the tree, which point towards the heavens, and laying them down on the earth to be trodden underfoot.

This link between heaven and earth is central to the Christian faith. It can be seen in the angel that appears to Mary and Joseph. In many artistic renderings of these encounters the hand of the messenger points up to God, as well as pointing out the task of the one who hears.

The events of Palm Sunday have been the subject of many great works of art. Artists use their hands to capture the excitement of the event and there are some common elements in many depictions of the scene. Duccio's *Entry into Jerusalem*, from the 14th century, is but one of a host of images that draw on the occasion. In that painting, as in many others that capture the scene, one of the hands of Jesus is raised in blessing. Some might think it the equivalent of a royal wave. The king on the donkey is giving a public acknowledgment of the presence of his subjects. Does this mean he may also be expecting some service?

In the other hand of Jesus are the reins with which he urges on the donkey to enter the holy city. The character of the donkey—a key player in the scene—is captured brilliantly in G.K. Chesterton's poem, which has the animal shirking off the image of

The devil's walking parody
On all four-footed things.

It concludes his account of that stunning parade by saying:

Fools! For I also had my hour;
One far fierce hour and sweet:
There was a shout about my ears,
And palms before my feet.

Not everyone is able to join in a processional re-enactment of the events remembered on Palm Sunday. Your church may not hold such an event. You may be constrained by health or responsibilities that make involvement in such a parade, no matter how attractive, either difficult or even impossible. That is not to say you cannot join such activity using your imagination.

It is a powerful and prayerful exercise to imagine ourselves in the scene. By reading the scene and placing ourselves in the crowd, we can enter more deeply into the atmosphere of that heady entry into the holy city. It can also be done by using our imagination to become one of the characters in a painting. That is the purpose of the exercises at the end of this chapter: to bring to life the images and events of Palm Sunday.

Those who join in the worshipful processions on Palm Sunday, whether by active participation or imagination, make their hands ready for the work of the rest of Holy Week. By lifting holy hands in worship, they are ready to greet their King. When the procession returns to the church there will often follow the first reading of the passion from one of the Gospels, capturing the story of the suffering and death of Jesus. The jubilant party atmosphere of the walk of witness transforms into the sombre reality of what was to happen to Jesus.

We know that the hands of Jesus, raised in blessing on Palm Sunday, will teach us other lessons and we will reflect on them in the following chapters. Among other things, the hands of Jesus will become an example of service. As disciples, we will be told to go and follow that example. The hands raised in blessing on Palm Sunday are the same ones by which Jesus gives himself to his followers in the form of broken bread. Those same hands are pinned to the cross for us on Good Friday. Those healing and commanding hands will be broken. The mystery and wonder is that despite and through all that destruction, we will be made whole. 'By his wounds you have been healed' (1 Peter 2:24).

God has no hands but our hands. Are our hands simply those that will be raised into the air when life is going well? Will our hands be absent from the more sombre observances, devoted to the pain and suffering of Jesus, where Christ extends his hands to us during Holy Week? Where will our hands be? Stretching toward Jesus in worship or leading us to a comfortable place to avoid where his hands are pointing?

Questions

1. What is your experience of Palm Sunday? What happens in your church? If you are in a group, you may want to discuss any similarities and differences.
2. If your church does not have a walk of witness on Palm Sunday, how might it benefit by having such a procession?
3. If your church does have one, how might it be improved?
4. Where might your hands be of use:
   ❖ in your church?
   ❖ in your workplace?
   ❖ in your community?

   Don't forget to give yourself credit for that which you are already doing!

Exercises

Choose one of the following exercises and spend some time pondering the questions.

1. Slowly read one of the Gospel accounts of the entry into Jerusalem (Matthew 21:1–9; Mark 11:1–10; Luke 19:28–38). Imagine yourself in the crowd. Ask yourself these questions:
   ❖ How does the palm/cloak feel in your hand?
   ❖ What is the weather like?
   ❖ What can you see… smell… taste?
   ❖ What emotions are you feeling? You may want to share them with others in the group.
   ❖ What can you see of Jesus?
   ❖ What would you like to say to Jesus as he rides past you?

   Slowly read the passage once again.

2. Find a picture of the scene. There are many images available on websites. Spend some time looking at the picture. Then imagine

yourself as one of the people in the scene. Closing your eyes may help. Then ask yourself the questions:

❖ How does the palm/cloak feel in your hand?
❖ What is the weather like?
❖ What can you see… smell… taste?
❖ What emotions are you feeling? You may want to share them with others in the group.
❖ What can you see of Jesus?
❖ What would you like to say to Jesus as he rides past you?

Look at the picture again.

Prayer

Almighty God,
who has given us hands to acclaim you in our world:
give us the energy to lift our hands
in worship and praise,
to applaud your wonder in our lives
and to offer our hands for the service of others.
Amen

NOTE

1 T.F. Hoad (ed.), *The Concise Oxford Dictionary of English Etymology*, Oxford, 1993, p. 332.

——— Chapter 6 ———

Go and do likewise

There is a tension about what we think is obvious and what we assume. The tension stems from what we think we can see and what we can learn from it. We find this kind of tension in pondering the notion of interaction between God's hands and his creation.

The tension takes on a special poignancy when we consider the events enshrined in the passion of Jesus. Those events are captured by many in the religious observances of Holy Week, which unfold around Jesus. Indeed, he is the very reason for both their happening and our subsequent consideration of them.

These events are inescapably bound up with the fundamental teaching of the Church—that Jesus was truly God and truly human. It cannot be overemphasized that his hands were human hands but they were also literally the hands of God. No wonder people longed to have these hands laid on them.

Followers of Jesus should not make light of this through over-familiarity. All too often we can turn his holy hands merely into a version of what we desire. We can run the risk of thinking they are only gentle, loving, healing hands. That is not in itself a bad thing, because there is no doubt that the hands were gentle, loving and healing.

'Let the little children come to me; do not stop them; for it is to such as these that the kingdom of God belongs. Truly I tell you, whoever does not receive the kingdom of God as a little child will never enter it.' And he took them up in his arms, laid his hands on them, and blessed them. (Mark 10:14–16)

However, the hands of Jesus should not be restricted solely to this kind of encounter. We have already reflected on the healing power in the hands of Jesus. We also saw the need to recognize reciprocity in those who reach out to Jesus, with Jesus reaching out to them.

In the events of the last supper those hands of Jesus are used to command his followers and also to command us. What Jesus does with his hands at this meal is worthy of deep and repeated consideration, even though, in some ways, it deals with what might be considered 'churchy' concerns. It can be argued that we need to be among fellow believers to do as Jesus commanded: to remember him in the breaking of bread and the sharing of a cup of wine. Remembering Jesus in this way should be a springboard for action.

For churches that observe Holy Week, the celebration of the Eucharist on Maundy Thursday is particularly striking. The celebration of Holy Communion is always an act of obedience, making real the command of Jesus to remember him in bread and wine. On Maundy Thursday many churches add to this regular ritual drama by enact-ing some other embodied teaching. In recreating some of the events captured in John's account of the last supper, we both recall what happened and are reminded of how we should act as followers of Jesus.

The first command is enshrined in the action usually known as the washing of the feet. It can be something of a fraught occasion in churches that re-enact it ritually. The task of the person planning the service involves the recruitment of twelve people to represent the apostles, who are willing to have someone, usually a member of the clergy, kneel in front of them and wash and dry their exposed feet. In some churches it is almost impossible to get the necessary number of volunteers. Those who are happy on other occasions to read, lead the prayers, preach or assist in the distribution of Holy Communion refuse to assume a role that means they need to uncover their feet in public.

Why do people shrink from it? The usual excuse is that people do not like others touching their feet. If that were the case, there would not be a chiropodist in business. There may be a more profound defence for the reluctant actors: perhaps their shyness stems from a realization of the implications of what the hands of Jesus did, which emerges from the verbal commentary that Jesus offered on his actions:

After he had washed their feet, had put on his robe, and had returned to the table, he said to them, 'Do you know what I have done to you? You call me Teacher and Lord—and you are right, for that is what I am. So if I, your Lord and Teacher, have washed your feet, you also ought to wash one another's feet. For I have set you an example, that you also should do as I have done to you.' (John 13:12–15)

Of course, the reluctant participants in this liturgy may be literalists. They simply may not be keen to go around washing other people's bared feet. Or they might have grasped the uncomfortable inversion of Christian living to which the words of Jesus point: those at the top should be at the bottom. That is not a particularly powerful place to be. 'Very truly, I tell you, servants are not greater than their master, nor are messengers greater than the one who sent them. If you know these things, you are blessed if you do them' (vv. 16–17).

To make the point again: to live as Jesus commands is to do more than repeat mere hand gestures. His teaching has to become fully embodied. The action that involves hands on feet leads to a new way of living. It creates new structures, ones in which the leader is a servant. It is no wonder people do not want to remove their shoes and socks and submit to this kind of inversion.

What Jesus commends to the apostles and to us is life-changing. Jesus adds a spoken commentary to his actions, yet it comes in scripture only after his hands have illustrated the teaching. Action precedes talk. In liturgical celebrations of Maundy Thursday we hear the Gospel read and watch the actions of hands washing feet, giving us a unified message. They combine so that 'we declare to you what was from the beginning, what we have heard, what we have seen with our eyes, what we have looked at and touched with our hands, concerning the word of life' (1 John 1:1).

Such a declaration in our hearts should follow the reading of the 13th chapter of John's Gospel in the Maundy Thursday service and be underlined by the liturgical actions captured in the washing of the feet.

If we read the account in John's Gospel it seems that even those who are close to Jesus do not immediately grasp what is going on. Peter does not want his leader to act as a servant, to behave like someone doing the lowly work of washing feet. But what Jesus does and says amounts to his saying, 'No, this is the way it must be.' So Peter, despite his belief that he is getting the idea, still misses the point. He urges Jesus to take his illustration to the next stage. It is as if he says, 'Go on. Go the whole hog.' He asks Jesus to wash not just his feet, but his hands and head as well (John 13:9). Peter is trying to distinguish himself by taking a relatively more exalted place. He wants to be the one who has more than his feet washed but Jesus says that this is not necessary. Peter then realizes that having his feet washed is not to single him out as special. There is nothing extraordinary in being among other followers. As Jesus points out, the servant is certainly not greater than the master.

The Gospel of Luke orders events and teachings differently from John. A similar teaching is illustrated by Jesus choosing to draw attention to someone who would not normally be considered influential by his disciples.

An argument arose among them as to which one of them was the greatest. But Jesus, aware of their inner thoughts, took a little child and put it by his side, and said to them, 'Whoever welcomes this child in my name welcomes me, and whoever welcomes me welcomes the one who sent me; for the least among all of you is the greatest.' (Luke 9:46–48)

Followers of Jesus are shown by their master how to behave. Christians should act in this way towards each other: a teacher is a servant; a leader has lowly tasks to do. In our service we act for Christ and that service should be enough in itself, rather than given in the hope or expectation of reward or recognition. For example, many churches put great energy and resources into the selection and training of leaders. Some have what seems a very worldly view of their importance. Indeed, some claim special status and privileges because of their position in the church. The events of Maundy Thursday might provide them with material worthy of prolonged meditation.

The Church is right to be concerned with itself by selecting, training and deploying appropriate personnel for its tasks. But it is not enough for Christians to confine service to their churches. They should have broader concerns: we should look to our master who came to save the world. It is important that service should extend beyond the scope of fellow religious travellers. The teaching of Jesus challenges us here:

When the Son of Man comes in his glory, and all the angels with him, then he will sit on the throne of his glory. All the nations will be gathered before him, and he will separate people one from another as a shepherd separates the sheep from the goats, and he will put the sheep at his right hand and the goats at the left. (Matthew 25:31–33)

The separation is based on what has been done in life. It centres on examples of service: feeding others, providing them with drink, welcoming strangers, clothing the naked, caring for the sick, visiting the prisoner. Both the sheep who go to their reward and the goats who are cast out are told that in serving others, we serve Christ. 'Truly I tell you, just as you did it to one of the least of these who are members of my family, you did it to me' (v. 40).

On this basis Christians cannot relegate social issues, especially justice, to ancillary concern. They are the very stuff of faith. Christianity is a way of life, of living in the real world, engaging with other people. This needs to be recognized among believers and, having been recognized, worked upon. A church has to be a church engaged in social concerns. Charity is not to be reserved for initiatives that solely benefit other Christians. God's love pours out on the world and the Church has the task of showing the world the nature of God's love. A Christian is thus challenged to try to reflect that love in everyday life—in the way they live at home, at work and at leisure. It is a profound challenge.

The events of the last supper move on. The hands of Jesus are used to leave another memorial, again captured in services on Maundy Thursday. Indeed, as has been noted, they are recalled every time the church gathers to celebrate Holy Communion. After all, Jesus himself said that this was an act by which we should remember him. 'Then he took a loaf of bread, and when he had given thanks, he broke it and gave it to them, saying, "This is my body, which is given for you. Do this in remembrance of me"' (Luke 22:19).

The early Church took this instruction extremely seriously, as recorded in the book of Acts: 'They devoted themselves to the apostles' teaching and fellowship, to the breaking of bread and the prayers' (Acts 2:42). This gives the pattern for Christian worship in the same way as the washing of the disciples' feet gives an example for social action. Study, companionship, Holy Communion and prayer are the template for the gathering of the faithful.

Accounts of the last supper focus on the hands of Jesus. He picks up bread, raises his hands in blessing, breaks the bread and then passes it to his followers. The celebration of the presence of Jesus in the form of bread and wine, irrespective of church party lines or tradition, should be informed by the actions of Jesus. There is no one way to mark this great feast. It can be solemn, enhanced by music, ceremony and choreography, or it may be simple and meditative. What should be undertaken with care is the action of the hands. Whoever takes the role of Christ in the re-enactment should be aware of the privilege and responsibility of the task.

The care with which hands undertake tasks informs those who are nearby of the importance, or otherwise, of an event. A simple comparison with the preparation and serving of food is instructive. If cooks do not wash their hands before starting to prepare the ingredients, if they work in a dirty kitchen and throw food around with little regard to the meal, it is probably right to assume that their task, and the person who will eat as a result of it, mean little to them. On the other hand, good personal care and a clean kitchen can lead to thoughtful preparation and the eventual attentive serving of the diner.

Slapdash celebrations of Holy Communion, whatever the theological slant or church politics involved, are simply not good enough. The hands that are lifted in prayer should be used thoughtfully in the remembrance of the Lord. After all, hands will take the bread and place it into the hands of others. In taking bread, breaking it and passing it, Jesus gives us the memorial of his self. Bread becomes flesh for his followers, in the same way that the Word was made flesh in creation. God gives himself in a new form to be held in our hands. We take bread, break it and pass it among us. This is fundamental for Christians, not just a nice and good thing to do. It is, as Jesus tells us, the way to remember him.

The hands of God in Jesus have shown us how to serve each other and the world. Those same hands, in taking bread and wine, have shown us how to remember Jesus. His followers do this by extending their hands to receive the memorial in the form of bread and wine. The hands of Jesus point the way for our hands and to the tasks we have to assume for him.

Questions

1. What does your church do in the service of others?
2. How can Christians show their faith in their daily lives? In what ways do you show your faith:
   * at home?
   * at work?
   * at leisure?
3. What more could your church do to help those in need? Try to think of practical examples.
4. What can we learn from examples of service:
   * in our church?
   * in our community?
   * in the world?

5. What lessons might we learn from those who offer service:
   - ❖ in the secular setting?
   - ❖ whose faith is different to ours?
   - ❖ yet say they have no faith?

Exercises

1. Get a map of your local area. Mark on it the various projects that are being undertaken for others. These can be quite simple: pensioners' lunch clubs, youth projects, drop-in centres. Do not confine yourself to church activities. Do you note any areas of duplication? Are there any gaps to note? If in a group, you may want to discuss how those gaps can be filled.
2. If possible, ask a priest to come to the house and celebrate Holy Communion for your group. Try to notice the gestures of the priest's hands, especially if your usual worship tradition tends toward the informal.
3. Try to recall the way you receive Holy Communion (if you do). What do your hands say
   - ❖ to you?
   - ❖ to others?

Prayer

O teacher God,
whose hands in Jesus pointed the way for us:
help us to see you when we gather
to remember you in bread and wine;
show us how to use our hands
in service of the world and the Church;
give us strength to bring our worship
and our service together in the places we find ourselves.
Amen

——— Chapter 7 ———

The events of Jesus' last hours on earth are essential reading for the Christian. They should also be the stuff of meditation. Much teaching and doctrine about Jesus and his saving actions is based on his last hours. The Church may have disagreements about the details and mechanics of how it matters (you only have to say the word 'atonement' to see this) but all agree that the things done by and to Christ do matter. The last hours of Jesus are known as his passion and involve his walk from Pilate's seat of judgment to the grave. The path taken by Jesus is linked in scripture and tradition to the progression of a sacrificial lamb offered by the levitical priests in the Old Testament. The priest whose task it was to offer sacrifice for himself and on behalf of others had to be ritually clean and this involved specific washing. That is the significance of the text from Psalm 26: 'I wash my hands in innocence, and go around your altar, O Lord, singing aloud a song of thanksgiving, and telling all your wondrous deeds' (vv. 6–7).

Attention to such matters continues today among Orthodox Jews and Muslims. Care is given to the body to allow spiritual duties to be performed properly. The text from Psalm 26 involves two aspects: the element of water and journeying with a purpose. Water is literally on hand for most of those who live in the developed world. Water washing over our hands is a basic and common experience for those who live in the West. People turn on taps and water comes out. Sometimes it is even drinkable.

This contrasts starkly with conditions for people living in many other parts of the world. It should not be forgotten that, even today, people are forced to give over large parts of their day to walk miles, collect water and carry it back to their homes or communities. What some of us get with a flick of the wrist involves a great and entire body effort for others. They rise early in the morning to beat the heat of the sun, journey to get to a source of fresh or relatively clean water, fill containers and try not to spill a drop on the return trip. What remains is used for a variety of purposes common to the developing and rich worlds. They can drink it or cook and clean with the travelled water.

Water also forms the basis of much personal hygiene. This is borne out by education. Children are taught that washing hands is a good thing in general and that it should be done at specific times, such as after they go to the toilet. Soap or other cleaning agents can be used but many such products need water to be efficacious: they cannot work without external liquid. The message of care for oneself and respect for others encapsulates the old maxim: cleanliness is next to godliness.

This care for others can be witnessed in two areas of human activity: in the preparation of food and medical care. We make sure (or we should) that we wash our hands before eating. Those working with food are repeatedly urged to keep their hands clean. Many public authorities insist on separate sinks and taps for the washing of hands and similar facilities used in the preparation of food. Those in the medical professions scrub up before and after procedures. A doctor is trained to do this routinely. A doctor will wash her hands before and after any kind of examination. It minimizes the spread of infection, protecting both patients and practitioner.

It would be simplistic, however, to suggest that washing hands is seen only as beneficial. The very expression 'to wash one's hands of a matter' has other, arguably sinister, connotations. By declaring that a person is washing their hands of an issue, the speaker is effectively distancing herself from the consequences of a course of action. It is tantamount to saying, 'This is something I cannot or will not concern myself with. If you want to pursue this course of action, so be it. Whatever the result, it is on your own head.' The expression 'I am washing my hands of the entire business' carries a great deal of meaning, most of it negative.

In many ways the hand washing of Pontius Pilate, often the focus of attention at the first halt on the devotional walk known as the Stations of the Cross, might be construed as the prime example of the more sinister attitude. Many people have offered all sorts of reasons for the actions of Pontius Pilate: he felt politically outmanoeuvred; his own standing with his superiors was vulnerable; he needed to curry favour with the local religious leaders; he had a naïve belief in the power of his own authority; he was scared; he feared for his personal safety; he was cut off from the majority of his troops who were deployed in another part of the city. Whatever the cause, the governor was in the central role. The fate of Jesus was in his hands.

Pilate is on the judgment seat. After leading an inquisition, he says he is satisfied that he can find no reason to put Jesus to death. Indeed, he goes further than that: he declares Jesus innocent. The synoptic Gospels capture this in a brief interchange. Pilate asks Jesus if he is the king of the Jews. 'You say so,' Jesus replies. In Luke, he sends Jesus off to Herod (Luke 23:7). Eventually Pilate asks if he should release Jesus. The people reject the idea, choosing Barabbas in his stead. Pilate appeals to the crowd, which replies in no uncertain terms: 'Crucify him!' Pilate reluctantly agrees to do this and then performs what some see as his infamous action: 'So when Pilate saw that he could do nothing, but rather that a riot was beginning, he took some water and washed his hands before the crowd, saying, "I am innocent of this man's blood; see to it yourselves"' (Matthew 27:24).

He washes his hands not so much to get Jesus off his hands— though he does do that—as to make a point to the accusers of Jesus. Pilate's actions amount to his saying once again that he believes the accused is being put to death not by him but by the force of the crowd: 'I am innocent of this man's blood.'

It is an odd thing, given that Pilate says he does not believe Jesus should die and thinks him innocent, that he does have him flogged.

Those who may have seen Mel Gibson's film *The Passion of the Christ* will realize that scourging was no great spectator sport. Flogging in those times was a brutal business. The lash was often tipped with all sorts of metal, stones and sharp objects. It was a bloody undertaking and in the film it is almost unbearable to watch.

But I want to rewind the action of the passion a little. Are other hands involved in this spectacle? There are the accusing fingers of the crowd. Jesus has broken so many rules. He has offended the religious hierarchy. He has outraged the devout and the ordinary believer. He has cured on the sabbath day, attacked the leaders of synagogues and outraged the authorities of the temple. He has claimed equality with God. In the context of these events, it is no wonder people are pointing the finger at Jesus. It is easy to imagine hands clenched in fists, the outrage in the shaking of arms.

Jesus is the accused and, as such, he assumes a particular role in the drama. It is possible for the faithful to forget what was at stake. Christians look at the events in a fuller way, realizing the saving implications of the suffering of Jesus. Yet it is worth allowing ourselves to follow the events as though we were contemporary spectators. That way we become players in the action and we can find our thoughts and emotions changing with the events.

At one point during this encounter, in the account in the Gospel of John, there is an appeal to a seemingly sensible logic: if Jesus had not done anything wrong, he would not be before the governor. Pilate goes to the crowd and asks the nature of the accusation against Jesus. They answered, 'If this man were not a criminal, we would not have handed him over to you' (John 18:30).

There is a sense here of the expression 'There is no smoke without fire', often used when there is actually scant evidence to implicate people in alleged criminal activity. For many fine upstanding citizens in Jerusalem at the time of his trial, Jesus must have represented a major threat to their values and way of life, perhaps as daunting as what is usually referred to as terrorism today. In the face of this, individuals and governments can turn their backs on long-cherished traditions of evidence and fair trial, even to argue that torture is acceptable in such circumstances. Such a daunting threat, they argue, must be criminal.

When Pilate challenges the suggestion of criminality of Jesus, the crowd responds with a short-term desire. 'Pilate said to them, "Take him yourselves and judge him according to your law." The Jews replied, "We are not permitted to put anyone to death"' (John 18:31).

This interchange points to a double washing of hands. The crowd is clearly expressing its desire for the death of Jesus. They want to see him dead but they are constrained by their own traditions. They also want to wash their hands of implication in the reality of judgment by passing it up the legal chain to the governor. They seek to distance themselves from their own desires by asking Pontius Pilate to deliver the death penalty that they have already decided Jesus deserves.

Even in these circumstances, Jesus manages to subvert events. In his teaching he had often provoked surprise and outrage by overturning the expectations of the traditions and laws of society. He managed to shock people into understanding what was coming from their hearts. Rather than point the finger, he suggested that people should look inwards and examine personal motivation. In effect, Jesus says, 'Look to your heart, because what is there will lead to the actions of your body. Your hands will follow your heart's inclination.'

In Mark's Gospel some Pharisees challenge Jesus when they see that his followers do not wash their hands before eating. They point out that the disciples are not observing cherished traditions. Jesus responds, 'Hear me, all of you, and understand: there is nothing outside a man which by going into him can defile him; but the things which come out of a man are what defile him' (Mark 7:14–15, RSV).

When challenged later about this, Jesus is graphic. In some more modern translations, what comes out of us passes into the sewer (v. 19). Repeatedly Jesus urges his followers to ensure that their actions flow from their hearts. In this way they can find a balance:

Do not judge, and you will not be judged; do not condemn, and you will not be condemned. Forgive, and you will be forgiven; give, and it will be given to you. A good measure, pressed down, shaken together, running over, will be put into your lap; for the measure you give will be the measure you get back. (Luke 6:37–38)

The following verses should be a guiding light for Christians:

Why do you see the speck in your neighbour's eye, but do not notice the log in your own eye? Or how can you say to your neighbour, 'Friend, let me take out the speck in your eye', when you yourself do not see the log in your own eye? You hypocrite, first take the log out of your own eye, and then you will see clearly to take the speck out of your neighbour's eye. (vv. 41–42)

This is not just a matter of personal piety. We need to pause and reflect on what is on our own hands. Too often we are keen to point the finger at the guilt or sin on others' hands. Jesus would have it otherwise. We need to think of our actions as persons, groups, families, churches, communities, societies and nations. Having done so, we can then seek to wash our hands in the forgiving love of God.

Questions

1. List three occasions when you think you have washed your hands of a matter, when it has been for the good of yourself and others:
   ❖ personally.
   ❖ as a member of a group.
   ❖ as a nation.
2. Consider the same question for times when you think your decision has been to the detriment of yourself and others.

Exercises

1. Prepare a bowl and a jug of water, with a hand towel. Think of something that has happened recently that troubled you in some way. Now pour water over your hands while you say, 'By the washing of my hands, I give this matter to God.' Keep a minute's silence. If you are meeting in a group, take turns to do this.
2. Sit in silence for a few minutes. Recall the following (one member of the group can read the list for others).
   ❖ Things you would like to say sorry for.
   ❖ Things you would like to forgive others for.

Then read the following prayer from Psalm 51 together.

Prayer

Have mercy on me, O God,
according to your steadfast love;
according to your abundant mercy
blot out my transgressions.
Wash me thoroughly from my iniquity,
and cleanse me from my sin.
For I know my transgressions,
and my sin is ever before me.
Against you, you alone, have I sinned,
and done what is evil in your sight,
so that you are justified in your sentence
and blameless when you pass judgment.
Indeed, I was born guilty,
a sinner when my mother conceived me.
You desire truth in the inward being;
therefore teach me wisdom in my secret heart.
Purge me with hyssop, and I shall be clean;
wash me, and I shall be whiter than snow.
(Psalm 51:1–7)

✢

──────── Chapter 8 ────────

Helping hands (Part 1): Simon of Cyrene

The cross has been placed into the hands of Jesus. The Gospels variously recount that he was scourged and mocked before being given his burden to carry to Calvary. In the traditional Stations of the Cross, Jesus receives this instrument of torture to carry directly after Pontius Pilate's washing of his hands. While Pilate declares that he is innocent of the blood of Jesus, even today there are some who say that his hands are tainted.

There are many whose hands will be stained with Christ's blood on the way to Golgotha. Some of them, soldiers and workmen, will be involved along the path of the passion. On one level they are people who come into the narrative merely because they are doing their jobs. These rough hands will touch Jesus on the way. Although their hands may be hardened, we should not presume that these people's hearts are as well. They do not necessarily use their hands with malicious intent.

While not drawing back from the brutality involved (specific attention will be given to some of the harsher aspects later), I want to consider three incidents in which Jesus is touched in a helpful, caring or loving way. The incidents are captured consecutively in three of the Stations of the Cross, although I am not going to look at them in the order they are usually observed.

The first incident is usually captured in the fifth station. Biblically we have very little to go on here. The Gospels mention simply that a man, Simon of Cyrene, was pressed into assisting the ailing Christ. We are given the fullest detail in the Gospel of Mark: 'They compelled a passer-by, who was coming in from the country, to carry his cross; it was Simon of Cyrene, the father of Alexander and Rufus' (15:21).

This verse shows that the reporter has done a bit of research. He knows where Simon comes from. We read that he is a father and we learn the names of his children. These details give rise to some questions. Were the children with him? Was his unnamed wife there? Why was he in Jerusalem? Many speculate that he was a pilgrim on his way to the temple to offer sacrifices and to pray. He was someone going about a sacred duty who found himself caught up in another person's story.

Luke gives some more text with a couple of other details. He not only mentions Simon of Cyrene but adds that he was compelled to carry the cross; he had been seized and the cross was laid on him; he walked behind Jesus; behind Simon came a great multitude of people, with a specific mention of women (23:26–27).

There is much to be gained from considering Simon of Cyrene's part in the passion of Jesus. We may forget that people can, with little desire or planning, find themselves drawn into the middle of very public events. A young man walks into his school with a rifle and those around him find themselves in the forefront of public examination to answer the impossible question, 'Why?' Hands are wrung in confusion and pain. Fists are clenched in frustration and anger. Fingers are pointed in blame. Such times also give rise to surprising reactions. Hands can also be extended in comfort when disaster strikes.

In a worldwide catalogue of atrocities the most notable event in recent times for Londoners was the bombings on the Underground on 7 July 2005. The diversity of those who use public transport at peak hours was evident. People from different ethnic, social and religious backgrounds were all victims of the blasts. Many survivors remarked how such barbarous acts turned a culture of polite un-friendliness among travellers (travelling at close quarters requires a certain protection of personal space) into one of collaboration and assistance. Strangers in adversity put differences to one side to help each other.

Sometimes life-changing events need not be so catastrophic. There is always the possibility of sudden transformation lurking in our lives: a misjudged step on a kerb; a trip on a railway platform; a momentary distraction at the wheel of the car. Each of these lapses can result in dire consequences. We do not need to—indeed, should not—live our lives in fear but it is worth acknowledging that these are real potential dangers. To admit it is not to close down opportunities or options like some over-zealous health and safety officer. It is rather to acknowledge the reality of sudden change in any situation.

It is the potential of being drawn from the midst of a crowd that makes Simon of Cyrene's story so interesting. Whatever the detail, he is someone who found himself drawn from the sidelines of an event into the middle of the action, moved from the edge of the picture into its centre.

I often recall a story I was told by a fellow priest about a neighbourhood passion play. The students of a theological college in a provincial cathedral city had decided to put on their performance as they walked through a busy street market. They were making their way through the stallholders and shoppers—most of whom ignored them. This took some doing, as the man playing Jesus was dressed only in a loincloth and the soldiers were in Roman garb. It is safe to assume that this was not an everyday occurrence.

As the procession was making its way through the street, the man playing the part of Jesus was carrying the cross. His steps started to falter. Looking into a nearby shop window was a smartly dressed man, apparently shopping with his wife and children. Suddenly, one of the soldiers mounted the footpath. A hand went out and grabbed the man out of his family group with the words, 'Right, mate, you'll do.' With that, the man found himself carrying the cross. The onlookers were shocked. Suddenly a seeming stranger had become a major player in someone else's drama. It can be that quick and that easy.

Compelled or reluctant, Simon of Cyrene takes the cross into his hands. He takes the burden of Jesus and carries it for him. This does not have to be seen as an heroic or even noble act. It is an action that offers relief and, for that reason alone, it needs to be recalled.

For many years I worked as a crime reporter. I often used to find myself at the aftermath of gruesome events. When I arrived at the scene many people seemed to be doing something useful. They—police officers, fire fighters or ambulance crews—all had the real frontline work. But there would often be other people in the vicinity. They could range from local borough staff, crews from other emergency and support services, the Salvation Army, people offering food and drink, to priests and counsellors offering an open ear to people. Those in that network of services seem to have acquired a right to be present.

There is another layer of participant in these events, the one between those directly involved in the situation and the spectators. There can often be an intrusive quality about their presence. That was certainly part of my feelings when I worked as a young journalist. At times I would step back from my immediate circumstances and reflect on what I was doing. I considered myself someone whose motives were perhaps not the most noble. At the worst, they seemed almost prurient.

This is not intended to be a generalized attack on those who work in the news media. There is, however, a dichotomy involved. It is now possible for us to be witnesses at many events that once we would have considered remote or even private. Rolling news and current affairs programmes, 'reality television' and many of the popular interview shows give us access to other people's lives. At times it can risk becoming tantamount to a freak show. Perhaps our watching such programmes and enjoying them might be part of a problem.

However, our involvement does not have to be negative. It is worth remembering that we do not need to be in the front line of action to be of help. It is possible to be an effective support without skills or expertise. In England this is captured in the expression of being prepared to share a cup of tea with somebody. We may not even be able to do that but that does not mean we need to feel useless. What takes us from being spectators, people entertained by events elsewhere in the world, is our preparedness to engage with them: prayer, support of relief agency appeals or volunteer work, if we are nearby, provide vital links between the suffering of others and ourselves.

'Whoever does not bear his own cross and come after me, cannot be my disciple' (Luke 14:27, RSV). Simon of Cyrene was called on literally to carry the cross of Jesus. Our discipleship is one mediated by time and distance. Christians need to look for ways to carry the cross in their own time and communities. It is worth remembering that Jesus told his hearers that each had a cross to bear, not that they should try to carry his. We have our own.

Simon of Cyrene is valuable not so much for who he was or the concerns of his life. Indeed, as we have seen, there is very little in the Bible to go on. The reason Simon of Cyrene is important is that his life was changed by circumstances that nobody could have predicted. Going about whatever business he had, he found himself no longer a spectator but a participant. He became the bearer of another's burden. That burden was the cross, an instrument of torture and the symbol of salvation.

Many churches adopt a managerial style today. The leadership formulates the vision and a mission action plan is developed to roll out the whos and hows and whens of achieving the vision. People are allocated or recruited to fulfil the tasks that will lead to assessable work. Have the objectives been achieved? Have the targets been hit? A process of review, planning and action is set in train. While there is some value in this, there is also value in merely being available. In that way no greater plan is required than being around when someone else is in need.

An individual, family or group can benefit from the knowledge and reality that someone else cares for them. That can be achieved in simple ways: a church, or parts of it, can be open for private prayer; pastors or members of a church can offer drop-in sessions; someone may be available for contact or prayer. These services can provide an assurance that a burden is or can be shared. Their cross becomes our cross. In that, we follow the actions of Simon of Cyrene, who took into his hands the burden of the cross of Jesus.

Questions

1. Can you think of times today when people do bad things in the name of just doing their job?
2. Do you have aspects of work about which you feel uncomfortable? What are they? How might you change them?
3. What are some of the more pressing issues or problems:
    ❖ in your community?
    ❖ in your church?
    ❖ in our world?

    Is there something you could do in response? What might it be? How would you go about lending a hand?
4. What do you think is your cross? How do you bear it?

Exercise

Think of a 'normal' activity that you engage in: shopping, going to church, dropping the children off at school, going to the post office, having a haircut. Think about what is involved in getting to that activity: the places you pass, the route you take, things that catch your eye on the way. Just spend a little time with those thoughts.

- What is the weather like?
- Who is around you?
- Who are you with?
- How are you feeling?

Now, someone grabs your arm and gives you the one thing you don't want. Let it be yours. It doesn't have to be massive or mighty, just something you don't want at that moment.

- A call on your mobile?
- A sick child?
- A worried parent?
- A noisy neighbour?

Step back and look at the scene. Is this your cross? Do you push it back into another's hands or are you willing to take up your cross, take it in your own hands and, like Simon of Cyrene, follow after Jesus?

Prayer

O God,
the bearer of our burdens,
help each of us to carry our own cross.
Give us the strength to lay it aside from time to time,
so that we may be bold enough
to look at the burdens carried by others.
In seeing them, help us to join with them
as they continue in the paths set before them.
May we look to Jesus
so that we can be of use to others who look to us.
Amen

+‡+

——— Chapter 9 ———

Helping hands (Part 2): Veronica and Mary

This chapter will be given over to more reflection on actions that could be considered as somewhat softening the passion of Jesus. This is not to diminish the painful path that Christ trod on Good Friday. It is done to show that the hands around Jesus were not all necessarily raised in anger, brute force or abuse.

We will look at two incidents, both involving women. Of course, that is not to ascribe soft, helping hands to women alone but these two characters provide examples of gentleness in an otherwise fairly brutal passage in the holy city of Jerusalem. Once again, the incidents are drawn from the traditional 14 Stations of the Cross that make up the journey of Jesus from Pilate's judgment seat to the grave.

The name of the first woman is Veronica, a name that cannot be found anywhere in the Bible. That is probably enough for some people to reject the incident out of hand. As it has no basis in scripture, they say, it is not worthy of consideration. If we are prepared to admit it, however, it can provide much valuable material for prayer and meditation, offering a creative way of joining Jesus on his walk to Golgotha.

A cloth was used to wipe the sweat from the face of Jesus and it acquired the name 'Veronica'. The vernicle (a word that some say is a corruption of the name Veronica itself) or *sudarium* (Latin for 'napkin') are words that are also used for the cloth. The name Veronica comes from the Greek *veron ikon*, which means 'true image', so the 'Veronica' is the face of Jesus. The sixth Station of the Cross often portrays a woman holding the cloth in the moments just after she has wiped the face of Jesus. The cloth holds an impression of the face of Jesus. Over time the name used for the cloth moved to christen the woman holding it.

Looking upon the 'Veronica' was a very popular meditation in years gone by. Before the increasingly graphic quality of film making and sound effects (Mel Gibson's *The Passion of the Christ* is perhaps the most recent and most brutal of a long line), the faithful would use such a picture as the gateway to an imaginative encounter with the depth of the passion of Jesus.

The National Gallery in London, against advice and all the odds, mounted an exhibition in 2000 entitled *Seeing Salvation*, which featured images of Christ. The exhibition gave over sections of the gallery to various aspects of the image of Christ: Sign and Symbol, The Dual Nature, Passion and Compassion, Praying the Passion, The Saving Body and The Abiding Presence. It also featured an entire section of versions of the 'Veronica' entitled The True Likeness. What surprised some of those who worked on the exhibition (if not the gallery's director, Neil MacGregor, who is himself a Christian) was its extraordinary popularity. It attracted some of the largest numbers to any exhibition there for years.

The second shock lay in people's behaviour. Gallery staff remarked that some people just did not behave as they should have done in an art gallery. People would be so struck by what they saw that they would drop to their knees and pray in front of works of art in the midst of the crushing crowds. In doing so, they were, of course, do-ing something that had been done for ages. They did not care about those around them: they had come to see art and found themselves moved to pray. The art became a window to God. They looked at an image and found a link of faith: 'Christ did this for me'. Their response was one of adoration.

Many of the 'Veronicas' in art galleries started their exhibitionary life in churches. A fair number can still be found in churches around the world today. Some of them, however, became collectable and made their way into more secular settings. As *Seeing Salvation* proved, the change of setting does not limit their power.

It is worth mentally stepping back from the gallery images to ponder the possible scenario that gave rise to them. The original 'Veronica' was the image reputedly captured on the cloth by a woman in the crowd on the Via Dolorosa, a street in Jerusalem believed to have been walked by Jesus on his way to Calvary. Pilgrims to the holy land often make a devotional walk, sometimes behind a large cross, which passes through the Muslim quarter of the old city. The street may still be there but the cloth itself, if it ever existed, has long gone.

Try to place yourself on the edge of the crowd, watching a procession of men making their way to death in Jerusalem. One of the men is, of course, Jesus. What are you wearing? What is the weather like? Who is around you? You feel a movement among the crowd. A woman steps out from the ranks of spectators and makes her way towards Jesus as he toils up the hill towards Calvary. She has a cloth in her hands with which she wipes the sweat, blood and tears from the face of Jesus.

Much can be made of this gesture. Defiance can be read into her act as dares to step out from the crowd to minister to a man on whom the powers and population have turned their backs. Or it can be considered in a much more low-key way: she sees a man struggling and simply offers him help. It is akin to offering a hand to someone who has tripped over in the street.

This seeming polarity between boldness and the mundane is essential to our lives. It is true that there will be times of seemingly dramatic intervention. There is an occasional need for a believer to stand up to and resist an evil—even if it is a popular and accepted one—that shakes the fabric of home, community, even nation. It is worth remembering that faith is not excluded from the poison of human corruption. Evils committed under the banner of religion have involved race, nationalism, sexual orientation, money and power. They are manifested in prejudice, blind adherence to patriotic fervour, greed and corruption. It should also be held in mind that all such failings are not necessarily historical. They still occur to this day. Standing up and challenging such perversions of faith is essentially an act of compassion. We cannot be angry about injustice if we have no sympathy or feelings for those who are oppressed or subdued. Again, like the other interpretation of the 'Veronica', our actions can be simple, heartfelt, person-to-person gestures. They are personal rather than political. They are humane rather than polemical.

Whether large or small, we can enact that which was caught in the words attributed to Mother Teresa of Calcutta:

Prayer in action is love, and love in action is service. Try to give unconditionally whatever a person needs in the moment. The point is to do something (however small) and show you care through actions by giving your time. Sometimes this may mean doing something physical (such as we do in our homes for the sick and dying) or sometimes it may mean offering spiritual support for the shut-ins (those isolated and lonely in their houses).[1]

To that end we should be prepared to look on the face of Christ in other people. We also need to be bold enough to let others see the Christ in our own faces. By seeing Christ in each other in this way, we move faith from the realms of placid piety to radical engagement. It is both humbling and challenging.

Service is an effect of God's love. The 'Veronica' is a sign of God's love. The fact that the Word made flesh was prepared to walk the torturous road to Calvary, to suffer and die to set us free, is captured in an image. The Christian faith is not based on a remote idea: it has a face. It is a face of which we do not have a record, in terms of its exact features, but whose image can be seen in the faces of those around us.

Let us now move on to the final encounter. It is often captured in a hand going out to, or even touching the face of, Jesus as he stops under the weight of the cross on the way to the crucifixion. It is a woman's hand—his mother's.

The scene represented in the fourth Station is another one that cannot be found in the Bible, although it has perhaps a little more basis than Veronica. It is reckoned as being part of the journey of Jesus from the praetorium to the tomb because Mary is mentioned as being among those standing at the foot of the cross. She would have had to get from wherever she was to Golgotha, which now is in the middle of the old city of Jerusalem but then was outside the walls of the town.

The scene in which Mary meets her condemned son is rightly poignant. This woman's life was turned upside down when she accepted the will of God: 'Behold, I am the handmaid of the Lord; let it be to me according to your word' (Luke 1:38, RSV). She is now called on to accept the fate of watching the child she bore go to his death.

The hand that is extended to the face of Jesus is the hand that held him to her breast. It is the hand that soothed his tears as a child. It is the hand that would have wiped his bottom. It is also the hand that would have been raised in rebuke, although we have only one such incident in the Bible—on the occasion when the boy Jesus stayed in the temple while the family returned home from Jerusalem (Luke 2:41–51).

There was a wonderful production of *The Mysteries* staged by a company of actors from South Africa in London in 2002. One of its conceits was that the disciples learned the gumboot dance from Jesus. This was a dance in which he had displayed extraordinary skill as a child. As he practised this dance flawlessly during a scene at home in Nazareth, every now and then his mother would clip him over the ear. He would stop and give Mary a questioning glance. The response told the audience that her action was a loving rebuke. If others were to learn from him, it seemed to say, the God-child needed to make the dance look learnable.

We are called, first and foremost, to follow Jesus not because we can do great things. Perhaps we can and, if we do, we should give thanks to God. But Christ's call is extraordinary because it is not to unusually gifted people. Jesus called ordinary men from their work by the Sea of Galilee. Their transformation into apostles was not immediate and wonderful. It was a process of learning, of making mistakes, sometimes of doubts and fears. To see evidence of this we only need look at the stories that concern Peter. He misunderstood Jesus many times. His reactions are replete with enthusiasm and blinkered comprehension. There is no doubt that Peter was a real, flawed human being. We, too, can learn from Jesus in our normality.

Mary is revered by the church because she was drawn from the ordinary. Some believers are suspicious of the role of Mary in the life of the Church because of the accretions and excesses that surround her. Yet devotion to Mary begins in a simple place. It is in Mary that we see the revolutionary designs of God. It is because she, like so many others in God's plan, was taken from a place of normality and elevated to a place of exceptional grace. That is why Mary deserves a special place in the life of the Church.

God's hand was upon Mary. Through her, others were also brought to be part of God's plan. However, this plan is often disruptive. In Mary's encounter with her cousin Elizabeth, we can see the ramifications of his love for humanity: the proud scattered in the imagination of their hearts, the mighty put down from their thrones, the exalting of the lowly, the hungry filled with good things and the rich sent away empty (Luke 1:46–55). The normal becomes inverted. And the final inversion is here, when a woman's hand is extended to her son as he carries a cross to his death.

Questions

1. What examples of a 'Veronica' have you seen?
2. How did you think and feel when you imagined yourself in the crowd as Jesus passed by?
3. Is there someone you know who needs assistance? What form might that assistance take? Can you offer time or practical support to them?

Exercises

1. If you are in a group, break into twos. For two minutes be prepared:
   - ❖ to look at your partner.
   - ❖ to be looked at by your partner.
2. When you have finished, discuss what you saw and how you felt when you were:
   - ❖ looking.
   - ❖ being looked at.
3. If you are on your own, look at your face in a mirror. What do you see of your inner self in your reflection? What might others see?
4. Get a picture of a 'Veronica'. Sit in front of it in silence for about five minutes. Discuss what thoughts and feelings this may have given rise to.

Prayer

O God,
whose hands fashioned and made the world:
fashion us in your image,
that we may encounter Jesus in others
and that they may recognize him in us.
Strengthen our hands for service
in the name of him whose hands were pierced on the cross,
even Jesus Christ our Lord.
Amen

NOTE

1 *A Simple Path*, Rider Press, 1995, p. 110.

·⁘·

——— Chapter 10 ———

Nailing the hands of Jesus

This chapter will once again draw on the traditions of the Stations of the Cross. The hands of Jesus being nailed to the cross is the subject of the eleventh Station. It is both shocking and workmanlike. It is shocking because there is no way to avoid or draw back from the sheer brutality of the act. At the same time it is workmanlike because it is, after all, a job of work for someone. The brutality takes force and determination. It may have had to be done through gritted teeth but done it was.

This calls for a potentially disturbing imaginative act. For a moment I want you to place yourself in the worker's position. In your hand is a hefty hammer. Can you feel its weight? In the fingers of your other hand you hold a nail. Look to the ground in front of you. A man's hand is open on a piece of wood. It is your job somehow to bang that nail through another human being's hand.

Let us draw back from the scene for a moment. It is, after all, a shocking place to be. We should remember, it was unlikely that this task could be achieved alone. At the least, Jesus would have to be tied down to allow it to happen. Hands have held, pushed and jostled him on the way. They have stripped his clothes from him and they have placed him on the wood.

No doubt there is strain in the hand of the man wielding the hammer. He has three tasks: to hold the hand of Jesus in place, to knock the nail through his flesh and to ensure that the nail is fixed into the wood. It takes concentration and effort.

The struggling Jesus, despite his acceptance of his fate, would have reeled in pain. Perhaps his hand made a fist in an effort to minimize the shock or he may have involuntarily drawn it back to avoid what was happening. He would have shifted as the blows sent aching waves through his body. Other men, other hands, are used to pinion him in order to allow the work of the hammerer to be carried out as efficiently as possible.

Did you know that no Gospel account of the passion of Jesus mentions his being nailed to the cross on Calvary? It is an action that we assume because of the post-resurrection encounter with Thomas. When told by the disciples that he has missed seeing Jesus, risen from the dead, Thomas says, 'Unless I see the mark of the nails in his hands, and put my finger in the mark of the nails and my hand in his side, I will not believe' (John 20:25). The challenge is met. When Jesus appears again to the disciples, this time with Thomas in the midst of them, he fulfils his criteria and Thomas moves to a declaration of faith: 'My Lord and my God!' (v. 28).

The marks of the nails appear in many pictures of the post-resurrection Christ. His hands show the wounds and his side often has the gash where the lance pierced his side, spilling the water and blood after his death. One painting, *The Incredulity of Saint Thomas* by Caravaggio, captures in graphic detail the moment when Thomas places his finger deep into the wound of the resurrected Christ.

Blood from the body of the dying Jesus used to be a key motif in many hymns. It reflected a deep devotion that was centred on the transforming suffering of Christ on the cross. In his resurrected life, Jesus carries what Charles Wesley calls in his Advent hymn, 'Lo! He comes with clouds descending', 'those glorious scars'.

No matter the wonder of God's actions through the passion of Jesus, it is still difficult to accept Samuel Crossman's sentiment expressed in the hymn, 'My song is love unknown':

Yet cheerful he
To suffering goes,
That he his foes
From thence might free.

The modern mind baulks at the suggestion of Jesus being cheerful in these circumstances. In the late 1990s John Pearce, an evangelical priest approaching his retirement from ministry in the East End of London, wondered if his younger colleagues were actually afraid of the image of the blood of Christ. He suggested that many contemporary worship songs almost avoided this aspect of Jesus' suffering. The Christian cannot take such easy evasive action. For the faithful there is no doubt about the resolve of the Christ to accept suffering to provide freedom to the world. But would we go so far as to say that in these actions Jesus remained cheerful? Perhaps a popular meaning of the word has now changed but it is hard to imagine someone today using the term in the context of Crossman's hymn.

The Church proclaims the message of liberation through the Lord's death. Indeed, it does more than that. The declaration of Thomas becomes the declaration of the believer: 'my Lord and my God'. The Church also affirms that Jesus was truly God and truly man. Whatever the resolution in his mind, there was real and agonizing pain involved in carrying out his task.

Pain is of more than passing concern to Christians. One of the most challenging questions about faith goes something like this: if God is good and all-powerful, why does he allow suffering? People who raise this issue usually have a particular emphasis, often linked to the suffering and illness of young people, perhaps someone in their own family or someone they know. If the loving, good God we talk about is real, then how did he, why did he, allow *my* child, friend, relation to suffer? Sometimes it is not particularity but scale that impels their question. Why does God let all those children in Africa, in India, in the Middle East, suffer?

It is a good question. To be honest, it is one of the toughest to answer because there is no easy answer. It is broadly categorized as the 'problem of evil'. Many responses have been formulated to this real and perennial difficulty and it is beyond the scope of this book to consider those responses.

Real people living real lives touch us and they demand that we make some response. So, if our faith is going to be of any use, it has to address realities. And it does. The Christian faith insists that the body and suffering of Jesus were real. The fact remains that it was a real hand that was nailed to the cross.

The Psalms contain all human life—joy, despair, anger, hatred, sadness, bewilderment—and they capture this question in one word, the one we ourselves have been asking: 'Why?' It can feel like a very lonely question. As Jesus cries from the cross in the words of the psalmist: 'My God, my God, why have you forsaken me?' (Mark 15:34; Psalm 22:1).

Asking God 'Why?' is both a personal and a broader question. One question that is often raised with people of faith is why notorious evildoers seem to prosper when the righteous go about begging for bread. How is it that good people seem to be taunted and persecuted when the fat gluttons round about them seem to live on the high hog? Where is God when we need him? This is, of course, not the precise text of the Psalms but it does give something of their flavour.

Perhaps the obvious needs to be stated here once again. These questions are not only put to people of faith; they are also posed by people of faith. The way they are postulated goes something like this: 'I don't set out to cheat anybody, I try to live by my principles, I pray, I support the church and only bad things seem to happen to me.' Alternatively, they take this form: 'It says in the Bible that if I work hard and for good, God will reward me.' And the answer takes a similarly personal vein: 'Well, I have worked hard and I have tried hard and there is no reward for me.'

These themes are the stuff of the passion. As a man's hands are stretched open when they would want to close in pain, these questions are inevitable. Do we have a response to these perplexities?

The issues about bad things happening to good people are addressed by Jesus in his teaching. In Luke 13 Jesus is asked about the Galileans whose blood Pilate had mingled with sacrifices. His response does not evade the issue but it is both strident and confronting: 'Do you think that because these Galileans suffered in this way they were worse sinners than other Galileans? No, I tell you' (Luke 13:2). He goes on: 'Or those eighteen who were killed when the tower of Siloam fell on them—do you think that they were worse offenders than all the others living in Jerusalem?' (Luke 13:2, 4).

There are many modern examples, both specific and more general, which point to the same central question: the bombing of Hiroshima in 1945; tornadoes in the south of the United States of America; the tsunami in the Pacific in 2004; devastating fires or floods; the attacks on the Twin Towers in Manhattan in 2001; shootings in schools; the Bethnal Green tube disaster in 1943.

The response of Jesus to the issue is not really one of comfort. His statement reiterates what he often says during his teaching ministry—which is that to look to others is to avoid the issues with oneself. If we want to understand this, we must look into our hearts and minds and ask big questions. We must look to the inner person to answer the outer questions. We have considered this in the washing of Pilate's hands. But then Jesus gives his listeners this: 'No, I tell you; but unless you repent, you will all perish just as they did' (v. 5).

These words of Jesus confronted his listeners in the same way that they challenge us today. It almost appears that Jesus avoids the question in some way. Jesus points out, however, that God does not abandon us. The author of Psalm 139 tells us God is with us in good and bad times (v. 8). It is sometimes hard to appreciate that, especially if we are experiencing what seem to be profound troubles. Our ability to respond through prayer or action can flow from uncomfortable circumstances. Jesus points to an outward and an inward journey. We are directed to examine our own consciences instead of trying to understand the larger picture.

God, all-powerful and all-knowing, allows the revelation of himself, Jesus, to be nailed to the cross. His answer to the questions raised about suffering is not really an intellectual response and some would, no doubt, scoff at the answer the Christian faith provides. God's answer is this: Jesus, as one of us, became so much at one *with* us that he suffered. He was prepared to undergo the most brutal and agonizing pain as a gift and example to those who would follow him.

What can be drawn from this? We can be reassured that God is not remote from us. God knows about pain and suffering because he endured it and we are taught that he endured it for us. The problem of suffering is thereby removed from the intellectual to the existential. In his being, God knows what we live through because he has been to the worst edges of it.

We are often bewildered by the events we see happening in the world but it would seem that looking to Jesus will give us something to work on. This is not contained in a pat, easy answer that solves all our problems. On the contrary, it is something that we have to grasp with resolution, as Jesus resolutely faced the agony of the cross. By doing so, as God did in Jesus, we are emboldened to engage with the reality of our lives. This is not so much a one-off solution, but an at-oneness. After all, Jesus let his hands be pierced for us.

Questions

1. What have been the times of physical or spiritual difficulty in your life?
2. Was there anything or anyone who was of special help to you in your difficulty? What or who was it? How did it or they help?
3. Are there parts of your life now that are in need of healing? How might you bring your concerns to God? What might you do to ask others for help?

Exercises

1. If you are a member of a group and feel confident in doing so, share with others your response to the questions above.
2. On the evening of 1943, a total of 173 people—women, children and men—were killed as they made their way into a bomb shelter in the then unused Underground station of Bethnal Green in London. People believed a new kind of bomb was being dropped

on the city. They turned out to be mistaken, and the greatest number of civilian fatalities were in the crush that ensued. Perhaps one of the group can find out more from the Internet. Imagine yourself as one of the following:

❖ Someone in the crushing crowd.
❖ An emergency worker on the scene.
❖ One of the people awaiting news of a loved one.

What and how would you pray? Is there something practical you could do in the situation?

Prayer

Saving God,
whose hands in Jesus were nailed to the cross:
give us the strength to open our minds and hearts
to the suffering of those around us.
Give us the boldness to join our needs with theirs
as we struggle with the perplexities of pain and suffering
through which we are joined to Jesus in his passion.
We ask this through the same Jesus Christ
who lives and reigns with you
in the unity of the Holy Spirit.
Amen

——— Chapter 11 ———

Empowering hands that touch the cross

What follows in this chapter is something of a journey. It is inevitable that some travelling is required when we are following the steps of Jesus as he walks to Golgotha. Repeated prayerful meditation on the passion, and the focus the Church gives it in Holy Week, move the faithful through time and space. It is also an exercise in measuring how far we feel from the dynamic tragedy of the crucifixion. Our steps now lead us to a place to consider the transfigured failure that took place on Calvary, a location where much comes together. That place is at the foot of the cross.

A recurrent theme of this book is that the creative events of God in the world and in Jesus are not remote from our lives today. We are joined to them by faith. In that way the events on the hill outside Jerusalem can connect with our lives. The questions and exercises at the end of the chapters in this book have sought to help us make real those connections.

Our journey will take us to one place from which we can contemplate the cross and consider how it might affect our daily lives. Its locus is in the East End of London, just over a mile from the vibrant international financial centre known as the City. We are in a fairly run-down churchyard, looking at an 18th-century brick building. It was designed by George Dance the Elder, the same architect responsible for the Mansion House, a magnificent Georgian palace that serves as the official residence of the Lord Mayor of London and the venue of many civic functions and receptions in the City.

We walk up a ramp of grey and black terrazzo and enter through the glass doors that allow us to look in from the outside to the beautifully carved wooden cross on the east wall of the church. We are standing inside St Matthew's, Bethnal Green, the church I have served since 2000. We glance around the walls and see the Stations of the Cross. They are stunning works of art. The artist, Don Potter, was chosen for this job as part of the restoration of the church, which was bombed by the *Luftwaffe* in the Second World War. While portraying the enervating journey of Jesus towards death, the images are full of vigour and life.

We see the traditional 14 scenes that follow the events of Good Friday, starting with the washing of Pontius Pilate's hands. From there, Jesus takes the cross into his hands and heads towards Calvary. On the way a number of incidents occur: he meets a number of women, including his mother, falls three times, is stripped of his clothes and is nailed to the cross, dies and is laid in the tomb. In making this journey we have moved from the east end of the north wall, down and across the back of the church.

After a graphic image of three hands—one in the form of the traditional priestly blessing held out on to the wood of the cross and two others driving a nail through the victim's palm—we encounter something different. The twelfth Station, with its portrayal of the crucifixion, stands out from the others. It boasts many unique qualities, the most obvious being that it is larger than the rest.

The space that separates the three figures in the scene is actually the fabric of the wall. Two of the three stand. The third, in the middle, is pinioned to the cross. The artist has introduced an arresting facet to the scene. The Stations previous to this one have a sombre hue. Potter used varying heats by firing the kiln with wood to create contrasts in the glaze of the ceramics. In the twelfth Station, however, the instrument of torture is a piecework of golden mosaic. Hundreds of small glistening stones combine to create the lifeless wood that has turned into the tree of life.

The scene has an ambivalent quality: the torso of Jesus looks strong but his arms are pinned, his hands fixed. His head droops along his right arm. The arms, along with the crossbar of the crucifix that gleams behind it, form a canopy. It is hard to know whether Potter is portraying Jesus as weak and still alive or as already dead. On either side of the golden mosaic cross stand the mother of Jesus and the beloved apostle, John.

To the left is Mary. Her grief is such that she cannot or does not raise her eyes to the spectacle of her dying son. Many have meditated on this scene since its installation in 1961. There is much to ponder: the tortured son hanging in front of the tortured woman with her hands folded in on herself; the woman, who as a young girl accepted with open arms the challenge of God to conceive miraculously and bear a son, cannot look at her dying child.

In Don Potter's rendering of the scene Mary is present but is seemingly disconnected, involved in her own grief. John, on the right-hand side, appears similarly dejected. He looks to the earth beneath him but there is a wonderful element in his stance—an unusual and subverting element. While John looks away from the suffering figure of Christ, his right arm is extended and his hand touches the gold of the crucifix.

What can be read from this contact? Suppose that the man whose touch healed so many has given up the ghost. John has then taken on a life-giving and caring commission from his teacher. In the Gospel that bears his name, John is given the care of the mother of Jesus: 'When Jesus saw his mother and the disciple whom he loved standing beside her, he said to his mother, "Woman, here is your son." Then he said to the disciple, "Here is your mother." And from that hour the disciple took her into his own home' (John 19:26–27).

Even in the face of death, Jesus has the power to change lives. The responsibility of a mother's care, commonly considered to be the special task of an eldest son, is given to someone else. This incident is often seen in the context of its emotion: a man who, in the midst of his pain and near to death, still ensures the ongoing welfare of the mother he loves. And yet the scene has almost conflicting consequences: it can either empower or limit us.

The first consequence is simple. Mary is enshrined as chosen. God sent his angel to tell her of her election to a special place in God's plan for the world. '"Hail, O favoured one, the Lord is with you!" But she was greatly troubled at the saying, and considered in her mind what sort of greeting this might be' (Luke 1:28–29, RSV). The words from Jesus on the cross echo her special status. She is first given to be the bearer of God and later is given by God-made-man into the care of his followers. It is no surprise that Mary holds a special place in the life of the Church. As we saw in the previous chapter, it is the very ordinariness of Mary that commends her.

The challenge of this exchange is caught by Don Potter. John's hand is touching the cross. John has been sent out as the Church has been sent out. He has been given a task as the Church has been given a task. John's new responsibility is another version of the many commissions that Jesus gives those who would follow him.

The call to conversion involves more than prayerful meditation on the teachings and events of the life of Jesus. The Son of Man repeatedly tells his followers to take on tasks: to spread the good news, to do as the good Samaritan did, to love enemies, to wash each other's feet, to question claims of self-righteousness over the grace of God. His disciples have attempted, and still try, to do this with varying degrees of success.

It can sometimes seem that the Church, despite touching the cross, has failed to rise to Christ's commission. Instead of looking for ways to care, serve and show God's love, its members become increasingly concerned with matters that might be considered as internal politics. Instead of going out, people retreat into a private club, seemingly interested only in other members. John's commission was immediate. The person he had to care for was next to the cross where he himself was standing. Putting ourselves into his place, we may feel paralysed in the face of the challenges that the world presents. What can we do in the face of such forces which deprive the world of justice? How should we meet the sometimes complex and complicated needs of those we encounter as we play our part in the Church's outreach to the communities it serves?

There is a risk of drawing back because of the enormity of the task but this would be tantamount to turning the commission of Christ, whose hands are pinned to the cross, into a shackling restriction. Jesus gives his commission to those whose hands are free. Lassitude is both dangerous and subversive to the profession of the Christian faith. Yet it is also sometimes a necessary reality check for those who imagine that their faith, combined with their good works, will fundamentally change the course of human events. Our faith calls us to try. In some cases we may succeed. But Jesus offered warnings about the enormity of the task even as he urged that it should be done: 'For you always have the poor with you, and you can show kindness to them whenever you wish' (Mark 14:7).

The Church needs to ensure that it does not lose that empowering touch shown by John's hand reaching out to the cross. It needs to keep contact with the wood of the cross while acknowledging the issues it faces. The Church should be one organization that transcends the borders of wealth and self-interest. If Paul's metaphor of the body holds true, then the strong, the comfortable and wealthy should be supporting those who are weak, unsettled and poor. That way, action follows contact with the cross. Realizing this, we need to stand back and look, as people do when they view the twelfth Station of the Cross in St Matthew's, Bethnal Green. Having stood back, however, they must resist the temptation to stand still. Having realized the implications of the scene, they need to press on to action by going back out into the world to serve others.

Questions

1. What inspired you to become a Christian?
2. How did the behaviour of others encourage you?
3. How did the behaviour of others discourage you?
4. What is the response of your church:
    ❖ to needs in the local community?
    ❖ to needs overseas?
5. How your church's response be improved?

Exercises

1. If you are on your own, place a cross on the floor or on a table in front of you. Give yourself two minutes in silence, then say the prayer at the end of this chapter.
2. If you are in a group, pass a cross among you. Let each member look at it. When everyone has had a chance to view and touch it, place the cross in the middle of the group. Then have one member say the following prayer, to which others make the response, 'I take to the cross of Jesus.'

Prayer

All my hopes and joys
I take to the cross of Jesus.
All my fears and sadness
I take to the cross of Jesus.
All my delight and joy
I take to the cross of Jesus.
All my pain and suffering
I take to the cross of Jesus.
All the troubles of this community
I take to the cross of Jesus.
All the strife in the world
I take to the cross of Jesus.
All of all and all in all
I take to the cross of Jesus.
Amen

——— Chapter 12 ———

Do not hold on to me

There is a poignant emptiness in many churches between Good Friday and Easter Sunday which is often at risk of being overlooked. That comes as no surprise, as there is a lot to prepare for in the services that make up Maundy Thursday, Good Friday and the Holy Saturday vigil. After the stripping of the altars at the conclusion of the Thursday service, the church should remain in a pared-back state. The relatively sparse solemnities of Good Friday highlight this. In churches that are usually marked by pomp and ceremony, the services are relatively low-key and meditative.

Against and amidst a background of this seeming bareness, a lot of activity can take place. This belies the sombre atmosphere which should rightly reign until the wonderful celebrations that attend the resurrection. Many churches have teams of people working to make the church ready for the special services on Saturday night and Easter Sunday morning. This work involves polishing brass and the vessels used in Holy Communion. Flowers are brought in and arranged for the first time since the beginning of Lent. The Paschal candle is prepared to be carried into a darkened church. The font is made ready for initiation ceremonies and the renewal of baptismal vows.

Preparation is no bad thing but it runs the risk of rushing past the emptiness that can attend a death. Holy Saturday, the day after Good Friday, is rightly the time when Christians should be mindful of this. The body of Jesus has been taken down from the cross and laid in a tomb so that his corpse would not be on public display on the sabbath day.

People who have been recently bereaved often say they feel numb after a funeral. So much has occurred in a relatively short space of time. The fact of a death is overtaken by a flurry of activity: the death needs to be registered and there are often other administrative tasks involved. There is liaison with funeral directors, ministers, friends and relatives. The relative calm of the funeral service, where the bereaved confront the reality of their beloved in a coffin and encounter perhaps the full force of their emotions, can disturb them. They have been through so much and now they are left to deal with the new situation—life without that person.

Keeping oneself busy in such circumstances is sometimes described as displacement activity. By attending to business and domestic matters, people are able to avoid thoughts of loneliness and desolation. Many bereavement counsellors suggest that, while there is no harm in such activity, it is important that people should not constantly resort to doing things. Time and reflection are also vital. The realities need to be confronted and that can often best happen in stillness.

There are two possible paths for those preparing churches for Easter. One is to attend to the preparatory duties in a prayerful, relatively sombre way, embracing the grief that followers of Jesus need to recognize. While they know that the death of Christ brings freedom to the faithful, it was done at a price and this needs to be acknowledged. At the same time, there is an innate sense of excitement as we are reminded that the Christian faith provides us with an astonishing hope. The death of Jesus is no ordinary death. 'He himself bore our sins in his body on the cross, so that, free from sins, we might live for righteousness; by his wounds you have been healed' (1 Peter 2:24).

This hope contains something precious for Christians. While we live in what some call a vale of tears, God has given into our hands a key to understanding suffering. Pain and suffering are not remote from God: he understands these things because, in Jesus, he underwent the agony of scourging and crucifixion. Jesus accepted the cross into his hands for us and we rejoice in what was achieved by his actions.

Even in grief—although it may not feel like it at the time—a

Christian can see the power of victory over death that was revealed in the resurrection.

Blessed be the God and Father of our Lord Jesus Christ! By his great mercy he has given us a new birth into a living hope through the resurrection of Jesus Christ from the dead, and into an inheritance that is imperishable, undefiled, and unfading, kept in heaven for you, who are being protected by the power of God through faith for a salvation ready to be revealed in the last time. (1 Peter 1:3–5)

The wonder of the events of Christ's resurrection has presented visual artists with many challenges. How can they not only portray the different Gospel narratives but, at the same time, convey their power? Many have attempted to rise to this task.

There is a splendid rendering of Christ bursting from the tomb by the 15th-century artist Piero della Francesca. In his *Resurrection* an upright Jesus has one foot on the edge of the tomb, which is fairly Italianate in style. (That is no surprise to students of religious art. Painters often used local architecture, botany and dress to bridge any possible distance between the viewer and the events depicted.) The left hand of Jesus rests on his left knee as he is about to lift himself out of the grave. This postural quirk bears an odd resemblance to a man hoisting himself out of a swimming pool. His other hand is uplifted and is holding the flag of victory. For a moment it is possible to imagine that Jesus might push down on the pole to ease his journey out of the tomb back into the world. At the base of the tomb are four people, some of whom are undoubtedly soldiers. One has his face in his hands. Is he crying, stunned or collapsed? The other three are clearly asleep.

This would seem to be a depiction of part of Matthew's account of the resurrection. Soldiers were placed at the tomb to ensure that nothing went amiss but, when Mary Magdalene and the other Mary made their way to the tomb, 'suddenly there was a great earthquake; for an angel of the Lord, descending from heaven, came and rolled back the stone and sat on it. His appearance was like lightning, and his clothing white as snow. For fear of him the guards shook and became like dead men' (Matthew 28:2–4).

A more dramatic rendering, although one that seems to show what happened before the guards 'became like dead men', can be seen in the Sistine Chapel. In *The Resurrection of Christ* by the 16th-century painter Hendrick van den Broeck, a victorious Christ looks down to one side. His entire body is surrounded by a radiant cloud. His left hand holds what looks uncannily like a processional cross, to which the victory flag is attached. His right hand points to the sky. In all this, Jesus appears to be hovering about two feet above the tomb. One of the soldiers is making off at high speed into the distance. Two seek to cover themselves with their shields and one lies on the ground. These men, key witnesses to the event, will soon become as though dead and will play a key part in downplaying what they have seen.

While they were going, some of the guard went into the city and told the chief priests everything that had happened. After the priests had assembled with the elders, they devised a plan to give a large sum of money to the soldiers, telling them, 'You must say, "His disciples came by night and stole him away while we were asleep." If this comes to the governor's ears, we will satisfy him and keep you out of trouble.' So they took the money and did as they were directed. And this story is still told among the Jews to this day. (Matthew 28:11–15)

A third image comes from Assisi, a place of pilgrimage for many Christians. *Noli me tangere* is a fresco, the work of the artist Giotto di Bondone (c.1267–1337). In it, a radiant Christ steps back from a kneeling woman, his arm extended to her as she reaches out towards him with both hands. Two angels sit on the tomb and two more are flying above the gilt-edged Christ figure.

The woman is, of course, Mary Magdalene. The image is known by the Latin rendering of the words Christ says to her in John's Gospel. These words are sometimes translated as 'Do not touch me' but would be better rendered as 'Do not hold on to me'.

Mary Magdalene's reputation has always suffered from misunderstanding, denigration and outright fiction. Some of this has happened within the Church and some for pure entertainment value. The most recent, popular and questionable effort is Dan Brown's bestselling novel *The Da Vinci Code*. He is not alone in peddling ideas of her marriage to Jesus, of the couple moving to foreign parts and their being progenitors of a secret clan. Her legacy was also besmirched by either innocent or deliberate confusion of identity. She has been identified as the woman with the alabaster jar of ointment (Matthew 26:7; Mark 14:3; Luke 7:37). Indeed, the jar is a key to recognizing Mary Magdalene in paintings and stained-glass windows. This association is dubious, however, and is based on a possible confusion of incidents and personalities.

Mary Magdalene's story is a complex one. The Gospel of Luke records that seven demons were cast out of her. In the same verse the writer notes that she was among a number of women who, from their own means, kept Jesus and his band of followers on the road.

Soon afterwards he went on through cities and villages, proclaiming and bringing the good news of the kingdom of God. The twelve were with him, as well as some women who had been cured of evil spirits and infirmities: Mary, called Magdalene, from whom seven demons had gone out, and Joanna, the wife of Herod's steward Chuza, and Susanna, and many others, who provided for them out of their resources. (Luke 8:1–3)

It is thus clear that Mary Magdalene contributed to the travelling ministry of Jesus. But what really gives her stature is her place in the post-resurrection stories. Each of the Gospels is sure on one point: Mary Magdalene was a primary witness to the resurrection. While they vary as to the identities of the women who made their way to the tomb where the body of Jesus had been laid, all agree that Mary Magdalene was one of them.

The most detailed and personal encounter is that recorded in the 20th chapter of John's Gospel. Mary goes to the tomb alone and finds that the stone has been removed. She runs to Simon Peter and 'the disciple Jesus loved' to tell them that the body of Jesus has been taken away. They then run to the tomb and see the cloth in which the body had been wrapped. There is an intriguing yet compromised declaration of faith at this point. 'Then the other disciple, who reached the tomb first, also went in, and he saw and believed; for as yet they did not understand the scripture, that he must rise from the dead' (John 20:9). They then leave.

It is what happens next that is so affecting and is the focus of *Noli me tangere*. Mary is weeping as she bends to look into the tomb. She sees two angels sitting where the body of Jesus had been. They ask her why she is crying and she responds that someone has taken the body to an unknown place.

When she had said this, she turned round and saw Jesus standing there, but she did not know that it was Jesus. Jesus said to her, 'Woman, why are you weeping? For whom are you looking?' Supposing him to be the gardener, she said to him, 'Sir, if you have carried him away, tell me where you have laid him, and I will take him away.' Jesus said to her, 'Mary!' She turned and said to him in Hebrew, 'Rabbouni!' (which means Teacher). Jesus said to her, 'Do not hold on to me, because I have not yet ascended to the Father. But go to my brothers and say to them, "I am ascending to my Father and your Father, to my God and your God."' Mary Magdalene went and announced to the disciples, "I have seen the Lord'; and she told them that he had said these things to her. (vv. 14–18)

There are some points to note that distinguish the written text from Giotto's rendering of the scene in Assisi. One resides in Mary's turning to speak to Jesus. Before both occasions of her speaking to Jesus, it is mentioned that she turned. We can speculate as to the reason for this. Perhaps she was still looking at the empty tomb. She may have been dazzled by the appearance of the angels. It may be that she was uncomfortable as a woman on her own in the burial place.

Giotto has Mary on her knees, extending her arms directly to Jesus. What might be inferred by her action? The first is not too difficult to understand. If you found yourself looking at someone whom you thought had died, you would probably want to touch them. Why? The immediate reason would be to check that the one you believed dead was really alive. A simple touch would let you feel the warmth of the other's body. Another reason is more emotional. You would reach out to hug them in joy and relief.

These actions are constrained by Jesus who, in Giotto's fresco, appears to be starting to walk away, as though showing Mary that there is more to be done. There is, however, something generous and wise in what he says to her. He is not shrugging Mary off: he is giving her a task. It is more than simply saying 'Do not try to contain me.' Jesus is pointing to wider implications of the event in which Mary figures, because what Mary is seeing is something so big that it cannot be contained by her hands. To grasp at Jesus would be to belittle what is happening. By claiming him for herself, Mary Magdalene would severely limit the power of what has occurred. It is as if she is trying to hide it away. It would go against what Jesus wants Mary to do because, if she does not try to hold on to him, she is free to spread the news of this glorious encounter. And by doing that she would be sharing Christ's gift to the world—to give life in all its fullness.

Mary Magdalene is, of course, an evangelist. She is the apostle to the apostles, the evangelist to the evangelists. We have noted that Mary Magdalene is the only consistent witness to the resurrection across the four Gospels. It is she who encounters the risen Christ and it is she, in the Gospel of John, who is given the model of Christian living. She is not to hold on to him as a private belonging. She is not to hide the news away. She is not to gloat over her special privilege. She understands this and immediately goes to tell others the good news.

Mary Magdalene is the model Christian. She witnesses to the power of Christ in her life: as healer, teacher and miracle worker. She witnesses to the wonder of his coming back from the dead. She tells of his turning death into life, and mourning into joy. Not only is she privileged enough to see these things but she shows us what to do. With so great a joy, how can we dare hold it to ourselves? As the hymn says, we have a gospel to proclaim. We should go out into the world and show people—by the way we live, the work we do, simply by being who we are—what God has done for us. We should not selfishly hold on to it. We should be daring. We should show our faith to the world with open hands.

Questions

1. Do you have a favourite Gospel account of the resurrection? Which one is it? Why do you like it?
2. When did you last tell anyone about your faith in Jesus?
3. What might you do to share the good news with people around you?

Exercise

Place your open hands into a favoured position for prayer. Remain silent for a minute. Then say the following prayer.

Prayer

Into your hands, O Lord, I commend my spirit.
Amen

brf

Resourcing your spiritual journey

through…

- Bible reading notes
- Books for Advent & Lent
- Books for Bible study and prayer
- Books to resource those working with under 11s in school, church and at home

- Quiet days and retreats
- Training for primary teachers and children's leaders
- Godly Play
- Barnabas RE Days

For more information, visit the **brf** website at **www.brf.org.uk**